JAVASCRIPT AND WBEMSCRIPTING ASYNC

Working with GetAsync

Richard Thomas Edwards

CONTENTS

Getting Started..8

ASP Reports 11

    Begin Code 11

    Horizontal No Additional Tags..12

    Horizontal Using A Button..12

    Horizontal Using A ComboBox..12

    Horizontal Using A Div...13

    Horizontal Using A Link...13

    Horizontal Using A ListBox 14

    Horizontal Using A Span..14

    Horizontal Using A Textarea 15

    Horizontal Using A TextBox 15

    Vertical No Additional Controls...16

    Vertical Using A Button...16

    Vertical Using A ComboBox 17

    Vertical Using A Div..17

    Vertical Using A Link...17

    Vertical Using A ListBox...18

Vertical Using A Span 18

Vertical Using A Textarea 19

Vertical Using A TextBox 19

End Code 20

ASP Tables...21

Begin Code..21

function Write_The_Code()..21

Horizontal No Additional Tags 22

Horizontal Using A Button 22

Horizontal Using A ComboBox...22

Horizontal Using A Div 23

Horizontal Using A Link 23

Horizontal Using A ListBox...24

Horizontal Using A Span 24

Horizontal Using A Textarea...25

Horizontal Using A TextBox..25

Vertical No Additional Controls 26

Vertical Using A Button 26

Vertical Using A ComboBox...26

Vertical Using A Div 27

Vertical Using A Link 27

Vertical Using A ListBox...28

Vertical Using A Span 28

Vertical Using A Textarea..29

Vertical Using A TextBox..29

End Code 30

ASPX Reports 31

Begin Code..31

Horizontal No Additional Tags 32

Horizontal Using A Button 32

Horizontal Using A ComboBox...33

Horizontal Using A Div 33

Horizontal Using A Link 33

Horizontal Using A ListBox 34

Horizontal Using A Span 34

Horizontal Using A Textarea 35

Horizontal Using A TextBox 35

Vertical No Additional Controls 36

Vertical Using A Button 36

Vertical Using A ComboBox 37

Vertical Using A Div 37

Vertical Using A Link 38

Vertical Using A ListBox 38

Vertical Using A Span 38

Vertical Using A Textarea 39

Vertical Using A TextBox 39

End Code 40

ASPX TABLES 41

Begin Code 41

Horizontal No Additional Tags 42

Horizontal Using A Button 42

Horizontal Using A ComboBox 42

Horizontal Using A Div 43

Horizontal Using A Link 43

Horizontal Using A ListBox 44

Horizontal Using A Span 44

Horizontal Using A Textarea 45

Horizontal Using A TextBox 45

Vertical No Additional Controls 46

Vertical Using A Button 46

Vertical Using A ComboBox 46

Vertical Using A Div 47

Vertical Using A Link 47

Vertical Using A ListBox 48

Vertical Using A Span 48

Vertical Using A Textarea 49

Vertical Using A TextBox 49

End Code 50

HTA REPORTS 51

Begin Code 51

Horizontal No Additional Tags 51

Horizontal Using A Button 52

Horizontal Using A ComboBox 52

Horizontal Using A Div 53

Horizontal Using A Link 53

Horizontal Using A ListBox 54

Horizontal Using A Span 54

Horizontal Using A Textarea 54

Horizontal Using A TextBox 55

Vertical No Additional Controls 55

Vertical Using A Button 56

Vertical Using A ComboBox 56

Vertical Using A Div 57

Vertical Using A Link 57

Vertical Using A ListBox 57

Vertical Using A Span 58

Vertical Using A Textarea 58

Vertical Using A TextBox 59

End Code 59

HTA TABLES 60

Begin Code 60

Horizontal No Additional Tags 61

Horizontal Using A Button 61

Horizontal Using A ComboBox 61

Horizontal Using A Div 62

Horizontal Using A Link 62

Horizontal Using A ListBox..63

Horizontal Using A Span...63

Horizontal Using A Textarea...63

Horizontal Using A TextBox..64

Vertical No Additional Controls..64

Vertical Using A Button..65

Vertical Using A ComboBox..65

Vertical Using A Div..66

Vertical Using A Link...66

Vertical Using A ListBox..67

Vertical Using A Span..67

Vertical Using A Textarea..67

Vertical Using A TextBox...68

End Code...68

HTML REPORTS 69

Begin Code...69

Horizontal No Additional Tags...69

Horizontal Using A Button..70

Horizontal Using A ComboBox 70

Horizontal Using A Div..71

Horizontal Using A Link...71

Horizontal Using A ListBox...71

Horizontal Using A Span 72

Horizontal Using A Textarea...72

Horizontal Using A TextBox..73

Vertical No Additional Controls 73

Vertical Using A Button 74

Vertical Using A ComboBox..74

Vertical Using A Div 75

Vertical Using A Link 75

Vertical Using A ListBox 75

Vertical Using A Span 76

Vertical Using A Textarea 76

Vertical Using A TextBox 77

End Code 77

HTML TABLES 78

Begin Code 78

Horizontal No Additional Tags 78

Horizontal Using A Button 79

Horizontal Using A ComboBox 79

Horizontal Using A Div 80

Horizontal Using A Link 80

Horizontal Using A ListBox 80

Horizontal Using A Span 81

Horizontal Using A Textarea 81

Horizontal Using A TextBox 82

Vertical No Additional Controls 82

Vertical Using A Button 83

Vertical Using A ComboBox 83

Vertical Using A Div 83

Vertical Using A Link 84

Vertical Using A ListBox 84

Vertical Using A Span 85

Vertical Using A Textarea 85

Vertical Using A TextBox 85

End Code 86

Stylesheets 87

NONE 87

BLACK AND WHITE TEXT 88

COLORED TEXT 91

OSCILLATING ROW COLORS 94

GHOST DECORATED 97

3D 100

SHADOW BOX 106

7

Getting Started

THIS IS A BOOK OF CODE. It includes ASP, ASPX, HTA and HTML Reports and tables being generated by WbemScripting and Get to power them.

No book is perfect and I'm sure you will find the usual small coding issues a book of this size is naturally going to have.

Aside from that, both table and report type views are part of the source code and each of those use an assortment of controls. The core code is below:

```
var doneonce = new String;
doneonce="false";

var x=0;
var y=0;
var z=0;
var names = new Array();
var values = new Array();
var va = new Array();

function GetValue(Name, obj)
{
    var tempstr = new String;
    var tempstr1 = new String;
    var tName = new String;
    tempstr1 = obj.GetObjectText_(0);
```

```
var re = /"/g;
tempstr1 = tempstr1.replace(re , "");
var pos;
tName = "\t" + Name + " = ";
pos = tempstr1.indexOf(tName);
if (pos > -1)
{
  pos = pos + tName.length;
  tempstr = tempstr1.substr(pos, tempstr1.length);
  pos = tempstr.indexOf(";");
  tempstr = tempstr.substr(0, pos);
  tempstr = tempstr.replace("{", "");
  tempstr = tempstr.replace("}", "");
  if (tempstr.length > 13)
  {
    if (obj.Properties_(Name).CIMType == 101)
    {
      tempstr = tempstr.substr(4, 2) + "/" + tempstr.substr(6, 2) + "/" +
tempstr.substr(0, 3) + " " + tempstr.substr(8, 2) + ":" + tempstr.substr(10, 2) + ":" +
tempstr.substr(12, 2);
    }
  }
  return tempstr;
}
else
{
  return "";
}
}
function sink_OnObjectReady(objWbemObject, objWbemAsyncContext)
{

  var objEnum = new Enumerator(objWbemObject.Instances_());
  for(;!objEnum.atEnd(); objEnum.moveNext())
  {
    var obj = objEnum.item();
    var propset = obj.properties_;
    var propEnum = new Enumerator(propset);
    for(;!propEnum.atEnd();propEnum.moveNext())
    {
```

```
      var prop = propEnum.item();
      if (doneonce == "false")
      {
         names[x] = prop.Name;
         va[x] = GetValue(prop.Name, obj);
      }
      else
      {
         va[x] = GetValue(prop.Name, obj);
      }
      x++;
   }
   doneonce = true;
   values[y] = va
   x = 0;
   y++;
  }

}


var v=0;

var mysink = WScript.CreateObject("WbemScripting.SWbemSink", "sink_");
var l = new ActiveXObject("WbemScripting.SWbemLocator");
var svc = l.ConnectServer(".", "root\\cimv2",,, "MS-0409");
svc.GetAsync(mysink, "Win32_Process");
```

ASP Reports

```
function Write_The_Code()
{
    var ws = new ActiveXObject("WScript.Shell");
    var filename = ws.CurrentDirectory + "\\Win32_Process.asp";
    var fso = new ActiveXObject("Scripting.FileSystemObject");
    var txtstream = fso.OpenTextFile(filename, 2, true, -2);
    txtstream.writeline("<html xmlns=\"http://www.w3.org/1999/xhtml\">");
    txtstream.WriteLine("<head>");
    txtstream.WriteLine("<title>Win32_Process</title>");
    txtstream.WriteLine("</head>");
    txtstream.WriteLine("<body>");
    txtstream.WriteLine("<%");
    txtstream.WriteLine("Response.Write(\"<table cellpadding=2 cellspacing=2>\" &
vbcrlf)");
    txtstream.WriteLine("Response.Write(\"<tr>\" & vbcrlf)");
    for(var c = 0;c < names.length;c++)
    {
        txtstream.WriteLine("Response.Write(\"<th          style='color:darkred;font-
size:10px;font-family:Cambria, serif;' align='left' nowrap>" + names[c] + "</th>\"
& vbcrlf)");
    }
    txtstream.WriteLine("Response.Write(\"</tr>\" & vbcrlf)");
```

Horizontal No Additional Tags

```
for(var d = 0;d < values.length;d++)
{
    txtstream.WriteLine("Response.Write(\"<tr>\" & vbcrlf)");
    va = values[d];
    for(var c = 0;c < names.length;c++)
    {
        txtstream.WriteLine("Response.Write(\"<td          style='color:navy;font-
size:10px;font-family:Cambria, serif;' align='left' nowrap>" + va[c] + "</td>\" &
vbcrlf)");
    }
    txtstream.WriteLine("Response.Write(\"</tr>\" & vbcrlf)");
}
```

Horizontal Using A Button

```
for(var d = 0;d < values.length;d++)
{
    txtstream.WriteLine("Response.Write(\"<tr>\" & vbcrlf)");
    va = values[d];
    for(var c = 0;c < names.length;c++)
    {
        txtstream.WriteLine("Response.Write(\"<td          style='color:navy;font-
size:10px;font-family:Cambria, serif;' align='left' nowrap><input Type= button
value=\"\" + va[c] + \"\"></input></td>\" & vbcrlf)");
    }
    txtstream.WriteLine("Response.Write(\"</tr>\" & vbcrlf)");
}
```

Horizontal Using A ComboBox

```
for(var d = 0;d < values.length;d++)
{

    txtstream.WriteLine("Response.Write(\"<tr>\" & vbcrlf)");
```

```
    va = values[d];
    for(var c = 0;c < names.length;c++)
    {
        txtstream.WriteLine("Response.Write(\"<td style='font-family:Calibri, Sans-
Serif;font-size: 12px;color:navy;' align='left' nowrap='true'><select><option value =
'"" + va[c] + "'>" + va[c] + "</option></select></td>\" + vbcrlf)");
    }
    txtstream.WriteLine("Response.Write(\"</tr>\" & vbcrlf)");
}
```

Horizontal Using A Div

```
for(var d = 0;d < values.length;d++)
{
        txtstream.WriteLine("Response.Write(\"<tr>\" & vbcrlf)");
        va = values[d];
        for(var c = 0;c < names.length;c++)
        {

            txtstream.WriteLine("Response.Write(\"<td          style='color:navy;font-
size:10px;font-family:Cambria,  serif;'  align='left'  nowrap><div>" + va[c]  +
"</div></td>\" & vbcrlf)");

    }
    txtstream.WriteLine("Response.Write(\"</tr>\" & vbcrlf)");
}
```

Horizontal Using A Link

```
for(var d = 0;d < values.length;d++)
{
    txtstream.WriteLine("Response.Write(\"<tr>\" & vbcrlf)");
    va = values[d];
    for(var c = 0;c < names.length;c++)
    {
```

```
        txtstream.WriteLine("Response.Write(\"<td style='font-family:Calibri, Sans-
Serif;font-size: 12px;color:navy;' align='left' nowrap='true'><a href='" + va[c] +
"'>" + va[c] + "</a></td>\" + vbcrlf)");
        }
        txtstream.WriteLine("Response.Write(\"</tr>\" & vbcrlf)");
    }
```

Horizontal Using A ListBox

```
    for(var d = 0;d < values.length;d++

    {

        txtstream.WriteLine("Response.Write(\"<tr>\" & vbcrlf)");

        va = values[d];
        for(var c = 0;c < names.length;c++)
        {
            txtstream.WriteLine("Response.Write(\"<td style='font-family:Calibri, Sans-
Serif;font-size:      12px;color:navy;'      align='left'      nowrap='true'><select
multiple><option value = '" + va[c] + "'>" + va[c] + "</option></select></td>\" +
vbcrlf)");
        }
        txtstream.WriteLine("Response.Write(\"</tr>\" & vbcrlf)");
    }
```

Horizontal Using A Span

```
    for(var d = 0;d < values.length;d++

    {

        txtstream.WriteLine("Response.Write(\"<tr>\" & vbcrlf)");

        va = values[d];
        for(var c = 0;c < names.length;c++)
        {
            txtstream.WriteLine("Response.Write(\"<td                style='color:navy;font-
size:10px;font-family:Cambria, serif;' align='left' nowrap><span>" + va[c] +
"</span></td>\" & vbcrlf)");
        }
        txtstream.WriteLine("Response.Write(\"</tr>\" & vbcrlf)");
```

```
        }
```

Horizontal Using A Textarea

```
    for(var d = 0;d < values.length;d++

    {

        txtstream.WriteLine("Response.Write(\"<tr>\" & vbcrlf)");

        va = values[d];
        for(var c = 0;c < names.length;c++)
        {
            txtstream.WriteLine("Response.Write(\"<td          style='color:navy;font-
size:10px;font-family:Cambria, serif;' align='left' nowrap><textarea>" + va[c] +
"</textarea></td>\" & vbcrlf)");
        }
        txtstream.WriteLine("Response.Write(\"</tr>\" & vbcrlf)");
    }
```

Horizontal Using A TextBox

```
    for(var d = 0;d < values.length;d++

    {

        txtstream.WriteLine("Response.Write(\"<tr>\" & vbcrlf)");

        va = values[d];
        for(var c = 0;c < names.length;c++)
        {
            txtstream.WriteLine("Response.Write(\"<td          style='color:navy;font-
size:10px;font-family:Cambria, serif;' align='left' nowrap><input Type=text
value=\"\" + va[c] + \"\"\"></input></td>\" & vbcrlf)");

        }
        txtstream.WriteLine("Response.Write(\"</tr>\" & vbcrlf)");
    }
```

Vertical No Additional Controls

```
for(var c = 0;c < names.length;c++)
{
    txtstream.WriteLine("Response.Write(\"<tr><th        style='color:darkred;font-
size:10px;font-family:Cambria, serif;' align='left' nowrap>" + names[c] + "</th>\"
& vbcrlf)");
    for(var d = 0;d < values.length;d++)
    {
        va = values[d];
        txtstream.WriteLine("Response.Write(\"<td         style='color:navy;font-
size:10px;font-family:Cambria, serif;' align='left' nowrap>" + va[c] + "</td>\" &
vbcrlf)");
    }
    txtstream.WriteLine("Response.Write(\"</tr>\" & vbcrlf)");
}
```

Vertical Using A Button

```
for(var c = 0;c < names.length;c++)
{
    txtstream.WriteLine("Response.Write(\"<tr><th        style='color:darkred;font-
size:10px;font-family:Cambria, serif;' align='left' nowrap>" + names[c] + "</th>\"
& vbcrlf)");
    for(var d = 0;d < values.length;d++)
    {
        va = values[d];
        txtstream.WriteLine("Response.Write(\"<td         style='color:navy;font-
size:10px;font-family:Cambria, serif;' align='left' nowrap><input Type= button
value=\"\" + va[c] + \"\"></input></td>\" & vbcrlf)");
    }
    txtstream.WriteLine("Response.Write(\"</tr>\" & vbcrlf)");
}
```

Vertical Using A ComboBox

```
for(var c = 0;c < names.length;c++)
{
    txtstream.WriteLine("Response.Write(\"<tr><th        style='color:darkred;font-
size:10px;font-family:Cambria, serif;' align='left' nowrap>" + names[c] + "</th>\"
& vbcrlf)");
    for(var d = 0;d < values.length;d++)
    {
        va = values[d];
        txtstream.WriteLine("Response.Write(\"<td style='font-family:Calibri, Sans-
Serif;font-size: 12px;color:navy;' align='left' nowrap='true'><select><option value =
'" + va[c] + "'>" + va[c] + "</option></select></td>\" + vbcrlf)");
    }
    txtstream.WriteLine("Response.Write(\"</tr>\" & vbcrlf)");
}
```

Vertical Using A Div

```
for(var c = 0;c < names.length;c++)
{
    txtstream.WriteLine("Response.Write(\"<tr><th        style='color:darkred;font-
size:10px;font-family:Cambria, serif;' align='left' nowrap>" + names[c] + "</th>\"
& vbcrlf)");
    for(var d = 0;d < values.length;d++)
    {
        va = values[d];
        txtstream.WriteLine("Response.Write(\"<td            style='color:navy;font-
size:10px;font-family:Cambria,  serif;'  align='left'  nowrap><div>"  +  va[c]  +
"</div></td>\" & vbcrlf)");
    }
    txtstream.WriteLine("Response.Write(\"</tr>\" & vbcrlf)")
}
```

Vertical Using A Link

```
for(var c = 0;c < names.length;c++)
```

```
    {
        txtstream.WriteLine("Response.Write(\"<tr><th        style='color:darkred;font-
size:10px;font-family:Cambria, serif;' align='left' nowrap>" + names[c] + "</th>\"
& vbcrlf)");
        for(var d = 0;d < values.length;d++)
        {
            va = values[d];
            txtstream.WriteLine("Response.Write(\"<td style='font-family:Calibri, Sans-
Serif;font-size: 12px;color:navy;' align='left' nowrap='true'><a href='" + va[c] +
"'>" + va[c] + "</a></td>\" + vbcrlf)");
        }
        txtstream.WriteLine("Response.Write(\"</tr>\" & vbcrlf)");
    }
```

Vertical Using A ListBox

```
    for(var c = 0;c < names.length;c++)
    {
        txtstream.WriteLine("Response.Write(\"<tr><th        style='color:darkred;font-
size:10px;font-family:Cambria, serif;' align='left' nowrap>" + names[c] + "</th>\"
& vbcrlf)");
        for(var d = 0;d < values.length;d++)
        {
            va = values[d];
            txtstream.WriteLine("Response.Write(\"<td style='font-family:Calibri, Sans-
Serif;font-size:        12px;color:navy;'        align='left'        nowrap='true'><select
multiple><option value = '" + va[c] + "'>" + va[c] + "</option></select></td>\" +
vbcrlf)");
        }
        txtstream.WriteLine("Response.Write(\"</tr>\" & vbcrlf)");
    }
```

Vertical Using A Span

```
    for(var c = 0;c < names.length;c++)
    {
        txtstream.WriteLine("Response.Write(\"<tr><th        style='color:darkred;font-
size:10px;font-family:Cambria, serif;' align='left' nowrap>" + names[c] + "</th>\"
& vbcrlf)");
        for(var d = 0;d < values.length;d++)
```

```
  {
     va = values[d];
     txtstream.WriteLine("Response.Write(\"<td          style='color:navy;font-
size:10px;font-family:Cambria,   serif;'   align='left'   nowrap><span>" + va[c] +
"</span></td>\" & vbcrlf)");
  }
  txtstream.WriteLine("Response.Write(\"</tr>\" & vbcrlf)");
}
```

Vertical Using A Textarea

```
for(var c = 0;c < names.length;c++)
{
   txtstream.WriteLine("Response.Write(\"<tr><th        style='color:darkred;font-
size:10px;font-family:Cambria, serif;' align='left' nowrap>" + names[c] + "</th>\"
& vbcrlf)");
   for(var d = 0;d < values.length;d++)
   {
     va = values[d];
     txtstream.WriteLine("Response.Write(\"<td          style='color:navy;font-
size:10px;font-family:Cambria,   serif;'   align='left'   nowrap><textarea>" + va[c] +
"</textarea></td>\" & vbcrlf)");
   }
   txtstream.WriteLine("Response.Write(\"</tr>\" & vbcrlf)");
}
```

Vertical Using A TextBox

```
for(var c = 0;c < names.length;c++)
{
   txtstream.WriteLine("Response.Write(\"<tr><th        style='color:darkred;font-
size:10px;font-family:Cambria, serif;' align='left' nowrap>" + names[c] + "</th>\"
& vbcrlf)");
   for(var d = 0;d < values.length;d++)
   {
     va = values[d];
     txtstream.WriteLine("Response.Write(\"<td          style='color:navy;font-
size:10px;font-family:Cambria,   serif;'   align='left'   nowrap><input   Type=text
value=\"\" + va[c] + \"\"></input></td>\" & vbcrlf)");
```

```
    }
    txtstream.WriteLine("Response.Write(\"</tr>\" & vbcrlf)");
}
```

End Code

```
txtstream.WriteLine("Response.Write(\"</table>\" & vbcrlf)");
txtstream.WriteLine("%>");
txtstream.WriteLine("</body>");
txtstream.WriteLine("</html>");
txtstream.Close();

}
```

ASP Tables

Begin Code

function Write_The_Code()

```
{
    var ws = new ActiveXObject("WScript.Shell");
    var filename = ws.CurrentDirectory + "\\Win32_Process.asp";
    var fso = new ActiveXObject("Scripting.FileSystemObject");
    var txtstream = fso.OpenTextFile(filename, 2, true, -2);
    txtstream.writeline("<html xmlns=\"http://www.w3.org/1999/xhtml\">");
    txtstream.WriteLine("<head>");
    txtstream.WriteLine("<title>Win32_Process</title>");
    txtstream.WriteLine("</head>");
    txtstream.WriteLine("<body>");
    txtstream.WriteLine("<%");
    txtstream.WriteLine("Response.Write(\"<table     Border=1     cellpadding=2
cellspacing=2>\" & vbcrlf)");
    txtstream.WriteLine("Response.Write(\"<tr>\" & vbcrlf)");
    for(var c = 0;c < names.length;c++)
    {
        txtstream.WriteLine("Response.Write(\"<th          style='color:darkred;font-
size:10px;font-family:Cambria, serif;' align='left' nowrap>" + names[c] + "</th>\"
& vbcrlf)");
    }
    txtstream.WriteLine("Response.Write(\"</tr>\" & vbcrlf)");
```

Horizontal No Additional Tags

```
for(var d = 0;d < values.length;d++)
{
    txtstream.WriteLine("Response.Write(\"<tr>\" & vbcrlf)");
    va = values[d];
    for(var c = 0;c < names.length;c++)
    {
        txtstream.WriteLine("Response.Write(\"<td          style='color:navy;font-
size:10px;font-family:Cambria, serif;' align='left' nowrap>" + va[c] + "</td>\" &
vbcrlf)");
    }
    txtstream.WriteLine("Response.Write(\"</tr>\" & vbcrlf)");
}
```

Horizontal Using A Button

```
for(var d = 0;d < values.length;d++)
{
    txtstream.WriteLine("Response.Write(\"<tr>\" & vbcrlf)");
    va = values[d];
    for(var c = 0;c < names.length;c++)
    {
        txtstream.WriteLine("Response.Write(\"<td          style='color:navy;font-
size:10px;font-family:Cambria, serif;' align='left' nowrap><input Type= button
value=\"\" + va[c] + \"\"></input></td>\" & vbcrlf)");
    }
    txtstream.WriteLine("Response.Write(\"</tr>\" & vbcrlf)");
}
```

Horizontal Using A ComboBox

```
for(var d = 0;d < values.length;d++)
{
    txtstream.WriteLine("Response.Write(\"<tr>\" & vbcrlf)");
```

```
        va = values[d];
        for(var c = 0;c < names.length;c++)
        {
            txtstream.WriteLine("Response.Write(\"<td style='font-family:Calibri, Sans-
Serif;font-size: 12px;color:navy;' align='left' nowrap='true'><select><option value =
'" + va[c] + "'>" + va[c] + "</option></select></td>\" + vbcrlf)");
        }
        txtstream.WriteLine("Response.Write(\"</tr>\" & vbcrlf)");
    }
```

Horizontal Using A Div

```
    for(var d = 0;d < values.length;d++)
    {
        txtstream.WriteLine("Response.Write(\"<tr>\" & vbcrlf)");
        va = values[d];
        for(var c = 0;c < names.length;c++)
        {

            txtstream.WriteLine("Response.Write(\"<td        style='color:navy;font-
size:10px;font-family:Cambria,    serif;'   align='left'   nowrap><div>" + va[c] +
"</div></td>\" & vbcrlf)");

        }
        txtstream.WriteLine("Response.Write(\"</tr>\" & vbcrlf)");
    }
```

Horizontal Using A Link

```
    for(var d = 0;d < values.length;d++)
    {
        txtstream.WriteLine("Response.Write(\"<tr>\" & vbcrlf)");
        va = values[d];
        for(var c = 0;c < names.length;c++)
        {
```

```
        txtstream.WriteLine("Response.Write(\"<td style='font-family:Calibri, Sans-
Serif;font-size: 12px;color:navy;' align='left' nowrap='true'><a href='" + va[c] +
"'>" + va[c] + "</a></td>\" + vbcrlf)");
    }
    txtstream.WriteLine("Response.Write(\"</tr>\" & vbcrlf)");
}
```

Horizontal Using A ListBox

```
for(var d = 0;d < values.length;d++

{

    txtstream.WriteLine("Response.Write(\"<tr>\" & vbcrlf)");

    va = values[d];
    for(var c = 0;c < names.length;c++)
    {
        txtstream.WriteLine("Response.Write(\"<td style='font-family:Calibri, Sans-
Serif;font-size:    12px;color:navy;'    align='left'    nowrap='true'><select
multiple><option value = '" + va[c] + "'>" + va[c] + "</option></select></td>\" +
vbcrlf)");
    }
    txtstream.WriteLine("Response.Write(\"</tr>\" & vbcrlf)");
}
```

Horizontal Using A Span

```
for(var d = 0;d < values.length;d++

{

    txtstream.WriteLine("Response.Write(\"<tr>\" & vbcrlf)");

    va = values[d];
    for(var c = 0;c < names.length;c++)
    {
        txtstream.WriteLine("Response.Write(\"<td              style='color:navy;font-
size:10px;font-family:Cambria, serif;' align='left' nowrap><span>" + va[c] +
"</span></td>\" & vbcrlf)");
    }
    txtstream.WriteLine("Response.Write(\"</tr>\" & vbcrlf)");
```

```
}
```

Horizontal Using A Textarea

```
for(var d = 0;d < values.length;d++
{
    txtstream.WriteLine("Response.Write(\"<tr>\" & vbcrlf)");

    va = values[d];
    for(var c = 0;c < names.length;c++)
    {
        txtstream.WriteLine("Response.Write(\"<td          style='color:navy;font-
size:10px;font-family:Cambria,  serif;'  align='left'  nowrap><textarea>" + va[c] +
"</textarea></td>\" & vbcrlf)");
    }
    txtstream.WriteLine("Response.Write(\"</tr>\" & vbcrlf)");
}
```

Horizontal Using A TextBox

```
for(var d = 0;d < values.length;d++
{
    txtstream.WriteLine("Response.Write(\"<tr>\" & vbcrlf)");

    va = values[d];
    for(var c = 0;c < names.length;c++)
    {
        txtstream.WriteLine("Response.Write(\"<td          style='color:navy;font-
size:10px;font-family:Cambria,    serif;'    align='left'    nowrap><input    Type=text
value=\"\" + va[c] + \"\"></input></td>\" & vbcrlf)");

    }
    txtstream.WriteLine("Response.Write(\"</tr>\" & vbcrlf)");
}
```

Vertical No Additional Controls

```
for(var c = 0;c < names.length;c++)
{
    txtstream.WriteLine("Response.Write(\"<tr><th        style='color:darkred;font-
size:10px;font-family:Cambria, serif;' align='left' nowrap>" + names[c] + "</th>\"
& vbcrlf)");
    for(var d = 0;d < values.length;d++)
    {
      va = values[d];
      txtstream.WriteLine("Response.Write(\"<td        style='color:navy;font-
size:10px;font-family:Cambria, serif;' align='left' nowrap>" + va[c] + "</td>\" &
vbcrlf)");
    }
    txtstream.WriteLine("Response.Write(\"</tr>\" & vbcrlf)");
}
```

Vertical Using A Button

```
for(var c = 0;c < names.length;c++)
{
    txtstream.WriteLine("Response.Write(\"<tr><th        style='color:darkred;font-
size:10px;font-family:Cambria, serif;' align='left' nowrap>" + names[c] + "</th>\"
& vbcrlf)");
    for(var d = 0;d < values.length;d++)
    {
      va = values[d];
      txtstream.WriteLine("Response.Write(\"<td        style='color:navy;font-
size:10px;font-family:Cambria, serif;' align='left' nowrap><input Type= button
value=\"\" + va[c] + \"\"></input></td>\" & vbcrlf)");
    }
    txtstream.WriteLine("Response.Write(\"</tr>\" & vbcrlf)");
}
```

Vertical Using A ComboBox

```
for(var c = 0;c < names.length;c++)
{
    txtstream.WriteLine("Response.Write(\"<tr><th          style='color:darkred;font-
size:10px;font-family:Cambria, serif;' align='left' nowrap>" + names[c] + "</th>\"
& vbcrlf)");
    for(var d = 0;d < values.length;d++)
    {
        va = values[d];
        txtstream.WriteLine("Response.Write(\"<td style='font-family:Calibri, Sans-
Serif;font-size: 12px;color:navy;' align='left' nowrap='true'><select><option value =
'" + va[c] + "'>" + va[c] + "</option></select></td>\" + vbcrlf)");
    }
    txtstream.WriteLine("Response.Write(\"</tr>\" & vbcrlf)");
}
```

Vertical Using A Div

```
for(var c = 0;c < names.length;c++)
{
    txtstream.WriteLine("Response.Write(\"<tr><th          style='color:darkred;font-
size:10px;font-family:Cambria, serif;' align='left' nowrap>" + names[c] + "</th>\"
& vbcrlf)");
    for(var d = 0;d < values.length;d++)
    {
        va = values[d];
        txtstream.WriteLine("Response.Write(\"<td                style='color:navy;font-
size:10px;font-family:Cambria,   serif;'   align='left'   nowrap><div>"   +   va[c]   +
"</div></td>\" & vbcrlf)");
    }
    txtstream.WriteLine("Response.Write(\"</tr>\" & vbcrlf)")
}
```

Vertical Using A Link

```
for(var c = 0;c < names.length;c++)
{
```

```
txtstream.WriteLine("Response.Write(\"<tr><th        style='color:darkred;font-
size:10px;font-family:Cambria, serif;' align='left' nowrap>" + names[c] + "</th>\"
& vbcrlf)");
    for(var d = 0;d < values.length;d++)
    {
        va = values[d];
        txtstream.WriteLine("Response.Write(\"<td style='font-family:Calibri, Sans-
Serif;font-size: 12px;color:navy;' align='left' nowrap='true'><a href='" + va[c] +
"'>" + va[c] + "</a></td>\" + vbcrlf)");
    }
    txtstream.WriteLine("Response.Write(\"</tr>\" & vbcrlf)");
}
```

Vertical Using A ListBox

```
for(var c = 0;c < names.length;c++)
{
    txtstream.WriteLine("Response.Write(\"<tr><th        style='color:darkred;font-
size:10px;font-family:Cambria, serif;' align='left' nowrap>" + names[c] + "</th>\"
& vbcrlf)");
    for(var d = 0;d < values.length;d++)
    {
        va = values[d];
        txtstream.WriteLine("Response.Write(\"<td style='font-family:Calibri, Sans-
Serif;font-size:    12px;color:navy;'    align='left'    nowrap='true'><select
multiple><option value = '" + va[c] + "'>" + va[c] + "</option></select></td>\" +
vbcrlf)");
    }
    txtstream.WriteLine("Response.Write(\"</tr>\" & vbcrlf)");
}
```

Vertical Using A Span

```
for(var c = 0;c < names.length;c++)
{
    txtstream.WriteLine("Response.Write(\"<tr><th        style='color:darkred;font-
size:10px;font-family:Cambria, serif;' align='left' nowrap>" + names[c] + "</th>\"
& vbcrlf)");
    for(var d = 0;d < values.length;d++)
    {
```

```
    va = values[d];
    txtstream.WriteLine("Response.Write(\"<td          style='color:navy;font-
size:10px;font-family:Cambria, serif;' align='left' nowrap><span>" + va[c] +
"</span></td>\" & vbcrlf)");
    }
    txtstream.WriteLine("Response.Write(\"</tr>\" & vbcrlf)");
}
```

Vertical Using A Textarea

```
for(var c = 0;c < names.length;c++)
{
    txtstream.WriteLine("Response.Write(\"<tr><th          style='color:darkred;font-
size:10px;font-family:Cambria, serif;' align='left' nowrap>" + names[c] + "</th>\"
& vbcrlf)");
    for(var d = 0;d < values.length;d++)
    {
        va = values[d];
        txtstream.WriteLine("Response.Write(\"<td          style='color:navy;font-
size:10px;font-family:Cambria, serif;' align='left' nowrap><textarea>" + va[c] +
"</textarea></td>\" & vbcrlf)");
    }
    txtstream.WriteLine("Response.Write(\"</tr>\" & vbcrlf)");
}
```

Vertical Using A TextBox

```
for(var c = 0;c < names.length;c++)
{
    txtstream.WriteLine("Response.Write(\"<tr><th          style='color:darkred;font-
size:10px;font-family:Cambria, serif;' align='left' nowrap>" + names[c] + "</th>\"
& vbcrlf)");
    for(var d = 0;d < values.length;d++)
    {
        va = values[d];
        txtstream.WriteLine("Response.Write(\"<td          style='color:navy;font-
size:10px;font-family:Cambria,   serif;'   align='left'   nowrap><input   Type=text
value=\"\" + va[c] + \"\"></input></td>\" & vbcrlf)");
    }
```

```
    txtstream.WriteLine("Response.Write(\"</tr>\" & vbcrlf)");
}
```

End Code

```
    txtstream.WriteLine("Response.Write(\"</table>\" & vbcrlf)");
    txtstream.WriteLine("%>");
    txtstream.WriteLine("</body>");
    txtstream.WriteLine("</html>");
    txtstream.Close();

}
```

ASPX Reports

Begin Code

```
var ws = new ActiveXObject("WScript.Shell");
var filename = ws.CurrentDirectory + "\\Win32_Process.aspx";
var fso = new ActiveXObject("Scripting.FileSystemObject");
var txtstream = fso.OpenTextFile(filename, 2, true, -2);
txtstream.writeline("<!DOCTYPE html PUBLIC \"-//W3C//DTD XHTML 1.0
Transitional//EN\"              \"http://www.w3.org/TR/xhtml1/DTD/xhtml1-
transitional.dtd\">");
txtstream.writeline("");
txtstream.writeline("<html xmlns=\"http://www.w3.org/1999/xhtml\">");
txtstream.WriteLine("<head>");
txtstream.WriteLine("<title>Win32_Process</title>");
txtstream.WriteLine("</head>");
txtstream.WriteLine("<body>");
txtstream.WriteLine("<%");
txtstream.WriteLine("Response.Write(\"<table              cellpadding=2
cellspacing=2>\" & vbcrlf)");
```

Horizontal Views

```
txtstream.WriteLine("Response.Write(\"<tr>\" & vbcrlf)");
```

```
for(var c = 0;c < names.length;c++)
{
    txtstream.WriteLine("Response.Write(\"<th        style='color:darkred;font-
size:10px;font-family:Cambria, serif;' align='left' nowrap>" + names[c] + "</th>\"
& vbcrlf)");
}
txtstream.WriteLine("Response.Write(\"</tr>\" & vbcrlf)");
```

Horizontal No Additional Tags

```
for(var d = 0;d < values.length;d++)
{
    txtstream.WriteLine("Response.Write(\"<tr>\" & vbcrlf)");
    va = values[d];
    for(var c = 0;c < names.length;c++)
    {
        txtstream.WriteLine("Response.Write(\"<td        style='color:navy;font-
size:10px;font-family:Cambria, serif;' align='left' nowrap>" + va[c] + "</td>\" &
vbcrlf)");
    }
    txtstream.WriteLine("Response.Write(\"</tr>\" & vbcrlf)");
}
```

Horizontal Using A Button

```
for(var d = 0;d < values.length;d++)
{
    txtstream.WriteLine("Response.Write(\"<tr>\" & vbcrlf)");
    va = values[d];
    for(var c = 0;c < names.length;c++)
    {
        txtstream.WriteLine("Response.Write(\"<td        style='color:navy;font-
size:10px;font-family:Cambria, serif;' align='left' nowrap><input Type= button
value=\"\" + va[c] + \"\"></input></td>\" & vbcrlf)");
    }
    txtstream.WriteLine("Response.Write(\"</tr>\" & vbcrlf)");
}
```

Horizontal Using A ComboBox

```
for(var d = 0;d < values.length;d++)
{
    txtstream.WriteLine("Response.Write(\"<tr>\" & vbcrlf)");
    va = values[d];
    for(var c = 0;c < names.length;c++)
    {
        txtstream.WriteLine("Response.Write(\"<td style='font-family:Calibri, Sans-
Serif,font-size: 12px;color:navy;' align='left' nowrap='true'><select><option value =
'" + va[c] + "'>" + va[c] + "</option></select></td>\" + vbcrlf)");
    }
    txtstream.WriteLine("Response.Write(\"</tr>\" & vbcrlf)");
}
```

Horizontal Using A Div

```
for(var d = 0;d < values.length;d++)
{
        txtstream.WriteLine("Response.Write(\"<tr>\" & vbcrlf)");
        va = values[d];
        for(var c = 0;c < names.length;c++)
        {

        txtstream.WriteLine("Response.Write(\"<td        style='color:navy;font-
size:10px;font-family:Cambria,   serif;'   align='left'   nowrap><div>" + va[c] +
"</div></td>\" & vbcrlf)");

        }
    txtstream.WriteLine("Response.Write(\"</tr>\" & vbcrlf)");
}
```

Horizontal Using A Link

```
for(var d = 0;d < values.length;d++)
{
    txtstream.WriteLine("Response.Write(\"<tr>\" & vbcrlf)");
    va = values[d];
    for(var c = 0;c < names.length;c++)
    {
        txtstream.WriteLine("Response.Write(\"<td style='font-family:Calibri, Sans-
Serif;font-size: 12px;color:navy;' align='left' nowrap='true'><a href='" + va[c] +
"'>" + va[c] + "</a></td>\" + vbcrlf)");
    }
    txtstream.WriteLine("Response.Write(\"</tr>\" & vbcrlf)");
}
```

Horizontal Using A ListBox

```
for(var d = 0;d < values.length;d++
{
    txtstream.WriteLine("Response.Write(\"<tr>\" & vbcrlf)");

    va = values[d];
    for(var c = 0;c < names.length;c++)
    {
        txtstream.WriteLine("Response.Write(\"<td style='font-family:Calibri, Sans-
Serif;font-size:    12px;color:navy;'    align='left'    nowrap='true'><select
multiple><option value = '" + va[c] + "'>" + va[c] + "</option></select></td>\" +
vbcrlf)");
    }
    txtstream.WriteLine("Response.Write(\"</tr>\" & vbcrlf)");
}
```

Horizontal Using A Span

```
for(var d = 0;d < values.length;d++
{
    txtstream.WriteLine("Response.Write(\"<tr>\" & vbcrlf)");

    va = values[d];
    for(var c = 0;c < names.length;c++)
```

```
    {
        txtstream.WriteLine("Response.Write(\"<td          style='color:navy;font-
size:10px;font-family:Cambria, serif;' align='left' nowrap><span>" + va[c] +
"</span></td>\" & vbcrlf)");
    }
    txtstream.WriteLine("Response.Write(\"</tr>\" & vbcrlf)");
}
```

Horizontal Using A Textarea

```
for(var d = 0;d < values.length;d++

{

    txtstream.WriteLine("Response.Write(\"<tr>\" & vbcrlf)");

    va = values[d];
    for(var c = 0;c < names.length;c++)
    {
        txtstream.WriteLine("Response.Write(\"<td          style='color:navy;font-
size:10px;font-family:Cambria, serif;' align='left' nowrap><textarea>" + va[c] +
"</textarea></td>\" & vbcrlf)");
    }
    txtstream.WriteLine("Response.Write(\"</tr>\" & vbcrlf)");
}
```

Horizontal Using A TextBox

```
for(var d = 0;d < values.length;d++

{

    txtstream.WriteLine("Response.Write(\"<tr>\" & vbcrlf)");

    va = values[d];
    for(var c = 0;c < names.length;c++)
    {
        txtstream.WriteLine("Response.Write(\"<td          style='color:navy;font-
size:10px;font-family:Cambria, serif;' align='left' nowrap><input Type=text
value=\"\" + va[c] + \"\"></input></td>\" & vbcrlf)");
```

```
    }
    txtstream.WriteLine("Response.Write(\"</tr>\" & vbcrlf)");
}
```

Vertical No Additional Controls

```
for(var c = 0;c < names.length;c++)
{
    txtstream.WriteLine("Response.Write(\"<tr><th        style='color:darkred;font-
size:10px;font-family:Cambria, serif;' align='left' nowrap>" + names[c] + "</th>\"
& vbcrlf)");
    for(var d = 0;d < values.length;d++)
    {
        va = values[d];
        txtstream.WriteLine("Response.Write(\"<td            style='color:navy;font-
size:10px;font-family:Cambria, serif;' align='left' nowrap>" + va[c] + "</td>\" &
vbcrlf)");
    }
    txtstream.WriteLine("Response.Write(\"</tr>\" & vbcrlf)");
}
```

Vertical Using A Button

```
for(var c = 0;c < names.length;c++)
{
    txtstream.WriteLine("Response.Write(\"<tr><th        style='color:darkred;font-
size:10px;font-family:Cambria, serif;' align='left' nowrap>" + names[c] + "</th>\"
& vbcrlf)");
    for(var d = 0;d < values.length;d++)
    {
        va = values[d];
        txtstream.WriteLine("Response.Write(\"<td            style='color:navy;font-
size:10px;font-family:Cambria, serif;' align='left' nowrap><input Type= button
value=\"\" + va[c] + \"\"></input></td>\" & vbcrlf)");
    }
    txtstream.WriteLine("Response.Write(\"</tr>\" & vbcrlf)");
```

```
        }
```

Vertical Using A ComboBox

```
    for(var c = 0;c < names.length;c++)
    {
        txtstream.WriteLine("Response.Write(\"<tr><th        style='color:darkred;font-
size:10px;font-family:Cambria, serif;' align='left' nowrap>" + names[c] + "</th>\"
& vbcrlf)");
        for(var d = 0;d < values.length;d++)
        {
          va = values[d];
          txtstream.WriteLine("Response.Write(\"<td style='font-family:Calibri, Sans-
Serif;font-size: 12px;color:navy;' align='left' nowrap='true'><select><option value =
'" + va[c] + "'>" + va[c] + "</option></select></td>\" + vbcrlf)");
        }
        txtstream.WriteLine("Response.Write(\"</tr>\" & vbcrlf)");
    }
```

Vertical Using A Div

```
    for(var c = 0;c < names.length;c++)
    {
        txtstream.WriteLine("Response.Write(\"<tr><th        style='color:darkred;font-
size:10px;font-family:Cambria, serif;' align='left' nowrap>" + names[c] + "</th>\"
& vbcrlf)");
        for(var d = 0;d < values.length;d++)
        {
          va = values[d];
          txtstream.WriteLine("Response.Write(\"<td        style='color:navy;font-
size:10px;font-family:Cambria, serif;' align='left' nowrap><div>" + va[c] +
"</div></td>\" & vbcrlf)");
        }
        txtstream.WriteLine("Response.Write(\"</tr>\" & vbcrlf)")
    }
```

Vertical Using A Link

```
for(var c = 0;c < names.length;c++)
{
    txtstream.WriteLine("Response.Write(\"<tr><th        style='color:darkred;font-
size:10px;font-family:Cambria, serif;' align='left' nowrap>" + names[c] + "</th>\"
& vbcrlf)");
    for(var d = 0;d < values.length;d++)
    {
        va = values[d];
        txtstream.WriteLine("Response.Write(\"<td style='font-family:Calibri, Sans-
Serif;font-size: 12px;color:navy;' align='left' nowrap='true'><a href='" + va[c] +
"'>" + va[c] + "</a></td>\" + vbcrlf)");
    }
    txtstream.WriteLine("Response.Write(\"</tr>\" & vbcrlf)");
}
```

Vertical Using A ListBox

```
for(var c = 0;c < names.length;c++)
{
    txtstream.WriteLine("Response.Write(\"<tr><th        style='color:darkred;font-
size:10px;font-family:Cambria, serif;' align='left' nowrap>" + names[c] + "</th>\"
& vbcrlf)");
    for(var d = 0;d < values.length;d++)
    {
        va = values[d];
        txtstream.WriteLine("Response.Write(\"<td style='font-family:Calibri, Sans-
Serif;font-size:      12px;color:navy;'      align='left'      nowrap='true'><select
multiple><option value = '" + va[c] + "'>" + va[c] + "</option></select></td>\" +
vbcrlf)");
    }
    txtstream.WriteLine("Response.Write(\"</tr>\" & vbcrlf)");
}
```

Vertical Using A Span

```
for(var c = 0;c < names.length;c++)
{
```

```
    txtstream.WriteLine("Response.Write(\"<tr><th        style='color:darkred;font-
size:10px;font-family:Cambria, serif;' align='left' nowrap>" + names[c] + "</th>\"
& vbcrlf)");
    for(var d = 0;d < values.length;d++)
    {
        va = values[d];
        txtstream.WriteLine("Response.Write(\"<td            style='color:navy;font-
size:10px;font-family:Cambria, serif;' align='left' nowrap><span>" + va[c] +
"</span></td>\" & vbcrlf)");
    }
    txtstream.WriteLine("Response.Write(\"</tr>\" & vbcrlf)");
}
```

Vertical Using A Textarea

```
    for(var c = 0;c < names.length;c++)
    {
        txtstream.WriteLine("Response.Write(\"<tr><th        style='color:darkred;font-
size:10px;font-family:Cambria, serif;' align='left' nowrap>" + names[c] + "</th>\"
& vbcrlf)");
        for(var d = 0;d < values.length;d++)
        {
            va = values[d];
            txtstream.WriteLine("Response.Write(\"<td            style='color:navy;font-
size:10px;font-family:Cambria, serif;' align='left' nowrap><textarea>" + va[c] +
"</textarea></td>\" & vbcrlf)");
        }
        txtstream.WriteLine("Response.Write(\"</tr>\" & vbcrlf)");
    }
```

Vertical Using A TextBox

```
    for(var c = 0;c < names.length;c++)
    {
        txtstream.WriteLine("Response.Write(\"<tr><th        style='color:darkred;font-
size:10px;font-family:Cambria, serif;' align='left' nowrap>" + names[c] + "</th>\"
& vbcrlf)");
        for(var d = 0;d < values.length;d++)
        {
```

```
        va = values[d];
            txtstream.WriteLine("Response.Write(\"<td                       style='color:navy;font-
size:10px;font-family:Cambria,   serif;'   align='left'   nowrap><input   Type=text
value=\"\" + va[c] + \"\"></input></td>\" & vbcrlf)");
        }
        txtstream.WriteLine("Response.Write(\"</tr>\" & vbcrlf)");
    }
```

End Code

```
    txtstream.WriteLine("Response.Write(\"</table>\" & vbcrlf)");
    txtstream.WriteLine("%>");
    txtstream.WriteLine("</body>");
    txtstream.WriteLine("</html>");
    txtstream.Close();

}
```

ASPX TABLES

```
function Write_The_Code()
{
    var ws = new ActiveXObject("WScript.Shell");
    var filename = ws.CurrentDirectory + "\\Win32_Process.aspx";
    var fso = new ActiveXObject("Scripting.FileSystemObject");
    var txtstream = fso.OpenTextFile(filename, 2, true, -2);
    txtstream.writeline("<html xmlns=\"http://www.w3.org/1999/xhtml\">");
    txtstream.WriteLine("<head>");
    txtstream.WriteLine("<title>Win32_Process</title>");
    txtstream.WriteLine("</head>");
    txtstream.WriteLine("<body>");
    txtstream.WriteLine("<%");
    txtstream.WriteLine("Response.Write(\"<table cellpadding=2 cellspacing=2>\" &
vbcrlf)");
    txtstream.WriteLine("Response.Write(\"<tr>\" & vbcrlf)");
    for(var c = 0;c < names.length;c++)
    {
        txtstream.WriteLine("Response.Write(\"<th          style='color:darkred;font-
size:10px;font-family:Cambria, serif;' align='left' nowrap>" + names[c] + "</th>\"
& vbcrlf)");
```

```
    }
    txtstream.WriteLine("Response.Write(\"</tr>\" & vbcrlf)");
```

Horizontal No Additional Tags

```
for(var d = 0;d < values.length;d++)
{
    txtstream.WriteLine("Response.Write(\"<tr>\" & vbcrlf)");
    va = values[d];
    for(var c = 0;c < names.length;c++)
    {
        txtstream.WriteLine("Response.Write(\"<td          style='color:navy;font-
size:10px;font-family:Cambria, serif;' align='left' nowrap>" + va[c] + "</td>\" &
vbcrlf)");
    }
    txtstream.WriteLine("Response.Write(\"</tr>\" & vbcrlf)");
}
```

Horizontal Using A Button

```
for(var d = 0;d < values.length;d++)
{
    txtstream.WriteLine("Response.Write(\"<tr>\" & vbcrlf)");
    va = values[d];
    for(var c = 0;c < names.length;c++)
    {
        txtstream.WriteLine("Response.Write(\"<td          style='color:navy;font-
size:10px;font-family:Cambria, serif;' align='left' nowrap><input Type= button
value=\"\" + va[c] + \"\"></input></td>\" & vbcrlf)");
    }
    txtstream.WriteLine("Response.Write(\"</tr>\" & vbcrlf)");
}
```

Horizontal Using A ComboBox

```
for(var d = 0;d < values.length;d++)
{
```

```
txtstream.WriteLine("Response.Write(\"<tr>\" & vbcrlf)");
va = values[d];
for(var c = 0;c < names.length;c++)
{
      txtstream.WriteLine("Response.Write(\"<td style='font-family:Calibri, Sans-
Serif;font-size: 12px;color:navy;' align='left' nowrap='true'><select><option value =
'" + va[c] + "'>" + va[c] + "</option></select></td>\" + vbcrlf)");
   }
   txtstream.WriteLine("Response.Write(\"</tr>\" & vbcrlf)");
}
```

Horizontal Using A Div

```
for(var d = 0;d < values.length;d++)
{
      txtstream.WriteLine("Response.Write(\"<tr>\" & vbcrlf)");
      va = values[d];
      for(var c = 0;c < names.length;c++)
      {

         txtstream.WriteLine("Response.Write(\"<td        style='color:navy;font-
size:10px;font-family:Cambria,   serif;'  align='left'  nowrap><div>" + va[c]  +
"</div></td>\" & vbcrlf)");

   }
   txtstream.WriteLine("Response.Write(\"</tr>\" & vbcrlf)");
}
```

Horizontal Using A Link

```
for(var d = 0;d < values.length;d++)
{
   txtstream.WriteLine("Response.Write(\"<tr>\" & vbcrlf)");
   va = values[d];
   for(var c = 0;c < names.length;c++)
   {
      txtstream.WriteLine("Response.Write(\"<td style='font-family:Calibri, Sans-
Serif;font-size: 12px;color:navy;' align='left' nowrap='true'><a href='" + va[c] +
"'>" + va[c] + "</a></td>\" + vbcrlf)");
```

```
    }
    txtstream.WriteLine("Response.Write(\"</tr>\" & vbcrlf)");
  }
```

Horizontal Using A ListBox

```
  for(var d = 0;d < values.length;d++

  {

    txtstream.WriteLine("Response.Write(\"<tr>\" & vbcrlf)");

    va = values[d];
    for(var c = 0;c < names.length;c++)
      {
        txtstream.WriteLine("Response.Write(\"<td style='font-family:Calibri, Sans-
Serif;font-size:   12px;color:navy;'   align='left'   nowrap='true'><select
multiple><option value = '" + va[c] + "'>" + va[c] + "</option></select></td>\" +
vbcrlf)");
      }
    txtstream.WriteLine("Response.Write(\"</tr>\" & vbcrlf)");
  }
```

Horizontal Using A Span

```
  for(var d = 0;d < values.length;d++

  {

    txtstream.WriteLine("Response.Write(\"<tr>\" & vbcrlf)");

    va = values[d];
    for(var c = 0;c < names.length;c++)
      {
        txtstream.WriteLine("Response.Write(\"<td            style='color:navy;font-
size:10px;font-family:Cambria,  serif;'  align='left'  nowrap><span>" + va[c] +
"</span></td>\" & vbcrlf)");
      }
    txtstream.WriteLine("Response.Write(\"</tr>\" & vbcrlf)");
  }
```

Horizontal Using A Textarea

```
for(var d = 0;d < values.length;d++
{
    txtstream.WriteLine("Response.Write(\"<tr>\" & vbcrlf)");

    va = values[d];
    for(var c = 0;c < names.length;c++)
    {
        txtstream.WriteLine("Response.Write(\"<td          style='color:navy;font-
size:10px;font-family:Cambria,  serif;'  align='left'  nowrap><textarea>" + va[c] +
"</textarea></td>\" & vbcrlf)");
    }
    txtstream.WriteLine("Response.Write(\"</tr>\" & vbcrlf)");
}
```

Horizontal Using A TextBox

```
for(var d = 0;d < values.length;d++
{
    txtstream.WriteLine("Response.Write(\"<tr>\" & vbcrlf)");

    va = values[d];
    for(var c = 0;c < names.length;c++)
    {
        txtstream.WriteLine("Response.Write(\"<td          style='color:navy;font-
size:10px;font-family:Cambria,   serif;'   align='left'   nowrap><input   Type=text
value=\"\" + va[c] + \"\"></input></td>\" & vbcrlf)");

    }
    txtstream.WriteLine("Response.Write(\"</tr>\" & vbcrlf)");
}
```

Vertical No Additional Controls

```
for(var c = 0;c < names.length;c++)
{
    txtstream.WriteLine("Response.Write(\"<tr><th         style='color:darkred;font-
size:10px;font-family:Cambria, serif;' align='left' nowrap>" + names[c] + "</th>\"
& vbcrlf)");
    for(var d = 0;d < values.length;d++)
    {
      va = values[d];
        txtstream.WriteLine("Response.Write(\"<td          style='color:navy;font-
size:10px;font-family:Cambria, serif;' align='left' nowrap>" + va[c] + "</td>\" &
vbcrlf)");
    }
    txtstream.WriteLine("Response.Write(\"</tr>\" & vbcrlf)");
}
```

Vertical Using A Button

```
for(var c = 0;c < names.length;c++)
{
    txtstream.WriteLine("Response.Write(\"<tr><th         style='color:darkred;font-
size:10px;font-family:Cambria, serif;' align='left' nowrap>" + names[c] + "</th>\"
& vbcrlf)");
    for(var d = 0;d < values.length;d++)
    {
      va = values[d];
        txtstream.WriteLine("Response.Write(\"<td          style='color:navy;font-
size:10px;font-family:Cambria, serif;' align='left' nowrap><input Type= button
value=\"\" + va[c] + \"\"></input></td>\" & vbcrlf)");
    }
    txtstream.WriteLine("Response.Write(\"</tr>\" & vbcrlf)");
}
```

Vertical Using A ComboBox

```
for(var c = 0;c < names.length;c++)
{
    txtstream.WriteLine("Response.Write(\"<tr><th          style='color:darkred;font-
size:10px;font-family:Cambria, serif;' align='left' nowrap>" + names[c] + "</th>\"
& vbcrlf)");
    for(var d = 0;d < values.length;d++)
    {
       va = values[d];
       txtstream.WriteLine("Response.Write(\"<td style='font-family:Calibri, Sans-
Serif;font-size: 12px;color:navy;' align='left' nowrap='true'><select><option value =
'" + va[c] + "'>" + va[c] + "</option></select></td>\" + vbcrlf)");
    }
    txtstream.WriteLine("Response.Write(\"</tr>\" & vbcrlf)");
}
```

Vertical Using A Div

```
for(var c = 0;c < names.length;c++)
{
    txtstream.WriteLine("Response.Write(\"<tr><th          style='color:darkred;font-
size:10px;font-family:Cambria, serif;' align='left' nowrap>" + names[c] + "</th>\"
& vbcrlf)");
    for(var d = 0;d < values.length;d++)
    {
       va = values[d];
       txtstream.WriteLine("Response.Write(\"<td               style='color:navy;font-
size:10px;font-family:Cambria,  serif;'  align='left'  nowrap><div>"  +  va[c]  +
"</div></td>\" & vbcrlf)");
    }
    txtstream.WriteLine("Response.Write(\"</tr>\" & vbcrlf)")
}
```

Vertical Using A Link

```
for(var c = 0;c < names.length;c++)
{
```

```
    txtstream.WriteLine("Response.Write(\"<tr><th        style='color:darkred;font-
size:10px;font-family:Cambria, serif;' align='left' nowrap>" + names[c] + "</th>\"
& vbcrlf)");
    for(var d = 0;d < values.length;d++)
    {
        va = values[d];
        txtstream.WriteLine("Response.Write(\"<td style='font-family:Calibri, Sans-
Serif;font-size: 12px;color:navy;' align='left' nowrap='true'><a href='" + va[c] +
"'>" + va[c] + "</a></td>\" + vbcrlf)");
    }
    txtstream.WriteLine("Response.Write(\"</tr>\" & vbcrlf)");
}
```

Vertical Using A ListBox

```
for(var c = 0;c < names.length;c++)
{
    txtstream.WriteLine("Response.Write(\"<tr><th        style='color:darkred;font-
size:10px;font-family:Cambria, serif;' align='left' nowrap>" + names[c] + "</th>\"
& vbcrlf)");
    for(var d = 0;d < values.length;d++)
    {
        va = values[d];
        txtstream.WriteLine("Response.Write(\"<td style='font-family:Calibri, Sans-
Serif;font-size:    12px;color:navy;'    align='left'    nowrap='true'><select
multiple><option value = '" + va[c] + "'>" + va[c] + "</option></select></td>\" +
vbcrlf)");
    }
    txtstream.WriteLine("Response.Write(\"</tr>\" & vbcrlf)");
}
```

Vertical Using A Span

```
for(var c = 0;c < names.length;c++)
{
    txtstream.WriteLine("Response.Write(\"<tr><th        style='color:darkred;font-
size:10px;font-family:Cambria, serif;' align='left' nowrap>" + names[c] + "</th>\"
& vbcrlf)");
    for(var d = 0;d < values.length;d++)
    {
```

```
    va = values[d];
    txtstream.WriteLine("Response.Write(\"<td        style='color:navy;font-
size:10px;font-family:Cambria, serif;' align='left' nowrap><span>" + va[c] +
"</span></td>\" & vbcrlf)");
    }
    txtstream.WriteLine("Response.Write(\"</tr>\" & vbcrlf)");
}
```

Vertical Using A Textarea

```
for(var c = 0;c < names.length;c++)
{
    txtstream.WriteLine("Response.Write(\"<tr><th        style='color:darkred;font-
size:10px;font-family:Cambria, serif;' align='left' nowrap>" + names[c] + "</th>\"
& vbcrlf)");
    for(var d = 0;d < values.length;d++)
    {
        va = values[d];
        txtstream.WriteLine("Response.Write(\"<td        style='color:navy;font-
size:10px;font-family:Cambria, serif;' align='left' nowrap><textarea>" + va[c] +
"</textarea></td>\" & vbcrlf)");
    }
    txtstream.WriteLine("Response.Write(\"</tr>\" & vbcrlf)");
}
```

Vertical Using A TextBox

```
for(var c = 0;c < names.length;c++)
{
    txtstream.WriteLine("Response.Write(\"<tr><th        style='color:darkred;font-
size:10px;font-family:Cambria, serif;' align='left' nowrap>" + names[c] + "</th>\"
& vbcrlf)");
    for(var d = 0;d < values.length;d++)
    {
        va = values[d];
        txtstream.WriteLine("Response.Write(\"<td        style='color:navy;font-
size:10px;font-family:Cambria, serif;' align='left' nowrap><input Type=text
value=\"\" + va[c] + \"\"></input></td>\" & vbcrlf)");
    }
```

```
    txtstream.WriteLine("Response.Write(\"</tr>\" & vbcrlf)");
}
```

End Code

```
txtstream.WriteLine("Response.Write(\"</table>\" & vbcrlf)");
txtstream.WriteLine("%>");
txtstream.WriteLine("</body>");
txtstream.WriteLine("</html>");
txtstream.Close();

}
```

Begin Code

```
function Write_The_Code()
{

   var ws = new ActiveXObject("WScript.Shell");
   var filename = ws.CurrentDirectory + "\\Win32_Process.hta";
   var fso = new ActiveXObject("Scripting.FileSystemObject");
   var txtstream = fso.OpenTextFile(filename, 2, true, -2);
   txtstream.writeline("<html>");
   txtstream.WriteLine("<head>");
   txtstream.WriteLine("<HTA:APPLICATION ");
   txtstream.WriteLine(" ID = \"Win32_Process\" ");
   txtstream.WriteLine(" APPLICATIONNAME = \"Win32_Process\" ");
   txtstream.WriteLine(" SCROLL = \"Yes\" ");
   txtstream.WriteLine(" SINGLEINSTANCE = \"yes\" ");
   txtstream.WriteLine(" WINDOWSTATE = \"normal\">");
   txtstream.WriteLine("<title>Win32_Process</title>");
   txtstream.WriteLine("</head>");
   txtstream.WriteLine("<body>");
   txtstream.WriteLine("<table  boder=0 cellpadding=2 cellspacing=2>\" & vbcrlf)");
```

Horizontal No Additional Tags

```
   for(var d = 0;d < values.length;d++)
```

```
    {
        txtstream.WriteLine("<tr>\" & vbcrlf)");
        va = values[d];
        for(var c = 0;c < names.length;c++)
        {
            txtstream.WriteLine("<td                style='color:navy;font-size:10px;font-
family:Cambria, serif;' align='left' nowrap>" + va[c] + "</td>");
        }
        txtstream.WriteLine("</tr>");
    }
```

Horizontal Using A Button

```
    for(var d = 0;d < values.length;d++)
    {
        txtstream.WriteLine("<tr>");
        va = values[d];
        for(var c = 0;c < names.length;c++)
        {
            txtstream.WriteLine("<td                style='color:navy;font-size:10px;font-
family:Cambria, serif;' align='left' nowrap><input Type= button value=\"\" + va[c] +
\"\"></input></td>");
        }
        txtstream.WriteLine("</tr>");
    }
```

Horizontal Using A ComboBox

```
    for(var d = 0;d < values.length;d++)

    {
        txtstream.WriteLine("<tr>");
        va = values[d];
        for(var c = 0;c < names.length;c++)
        {
```

```
        txtstream.WriteLine("<td    style='font-family:Calibri,    Sans-Serif;font-size:
12px;color:navy;' align='left' nowrap='true'><select><option value = '" + va[c] +
"'>" + va[c] + "</option></select></td>\" + vbcrlf)");
    }
    txtstream.WriteLine("</tr>");
}
```

Horizontal Using A Div

```
for(var d = 0;d < values.length;d++)
{
        txtstream.WriteLine("<tr>");
        va = values[d];
        for(var c = 0;c < names.length;c++)
        {

            txtstream.WriteLine("<td           style='color:navy;font-size:10px;font-
family:Cambria, serif;' align='left' nowrap><div>" + va[c] + "</div></td>");

    }
    txtstream.WriteLine("</tr>");
}
```

Horizontal Using A Link

```
for(var d = 0;d < values.length;d++)
{
    txtstream.WriteLine("<tr>");
    va = values[d];
    for(var c = 0;c < names.length;c++)
    {
        txtstream.WriteLine("<td    style='font-family:Calibri,    Sans-Serif;font-size:
12px;color:navy;' align='left' nowrap='true'><a href='" + va[c] + "'>" + va[c] +
"</a></td>\" + vbcrlf)");
    }
    txtstream.WriteLine("</tr>");
}
```

Horizontal Using A ListBox

```
for(var d = 0;d < values.length;d++

{

    txtstream.WriteLine("<tr>");

    va = values[d];
    for(var c = 0;c < names.length;c++)
    {
        txtstream.WriteLine("<td   style='font-family:Calibri,   Sans-Serif;font-size:
12px;color:navy;' align='left' nowrap='true'><select multiple><option value = '" +
va[c] + "'>" + va[c] + "</option></select></td>\" + vbcrlf)");
    }
    txtstream.WriteLine("</tr>");
}
```

Horizontal Using A Span

```
for(var d = 0;d < values.length;d++

{

    txtstream.WriteLine("<tr>");

    va = values[d];
    for(var c = 0;c < names.length;c++)
    {
        txtstream.WriteLine("<td              style='color:navy;font-size:10px;font-
family:Cambria, serif;' align='left' nowrap><span>" + va[c] + "</span></td>");
    }
    txtstream.WriteLine("</tr>");
}
```

Horizontal Using A Textarea

```
for(var d = 0;d < values.length;d++

{
```

```
txtstream.WriteLine("<tr>");

va = values[d];
for(var c = 0;c < names.length;c++)
{
    txtstream.WriteLine("<td                style='color:navy;font-size:10px;font-
family:Cambria,    serif;'    align='left'  nowrap><textarea>" + va[c] +
"</textarea></td>");
}
txtstream.WriteLine("</tr>");
}
```

Horizontal Using A TextBox

```
for(var d = 0;d < values.length;d++

{

    txtstream.WriteLine("<tr>");

    va = values[d];
    for(var c = 0;c < names.length;c++)
    {
        txtstream.WriteLine("<td                style='color:navy;font-size:10px;font-
family:Cambria, serif;' align='left' nowrap><input Type=text value=\"\" + va[c] +
\"\"></input></td>");

    }
    txtstream.WriteLine("</tr>");
}
```

Vertical No Additional Controls

```
for(var c = 0;c < names.length;c++)
{
    txtstream.WriteLine("<tr><th                style='color:darkred;font-size:10px;font-
family:Cambria, serif;' align='left' nowrap>" + names[c] + "</th>");
    for(var d = 0;d < values.length;d++)
    {
```

```
        va = values[d];
        txtstream.WriteLine("<td                 style='color:navy;font-size:10px;font-
family:Cambria, serif;' align='left' nowrap>" + va[c] + "</td>");
    }
    txtstream.WriteLine("</tr>");
}
```

Vertical Using A Button

```
for(var c = 0;c < names.length;c++)
{
    txtstream.WriteLine("<tr><th              style='color:darkred;font-size:10px;font-
family:Cambria, serif;' align='left' nowrap>" + names[c] + "</th>");
    for(var d = 0;d < values.length;d++)
    {
        va = values[d];
        txtstream.WriteLine("<td                 style='color:navy;font-size:10px;font-
family:Cambria, serif;' align='left' nowrap><input Type= button value=\"\" + va[c] +
\"\"></input></td>");
    }
    txtstream.WriteLine("</tr>");
}
```

Vertical Using A ComboBox

```
for(var c = 0;c < names.length;c++)
{
    txtstream.WriteLine("<tr><th              style='color:darkred;font-size:10px;font-
family:Cambria, serif;' align='left' nowrap>" + names[c] + "</th>");
    for(var d = 0;d < values.length;d++)
    {
        va = values[d];
        txtstream.WriteLine("<td    style='font-family:Calibri,   Sans-Serif;font-size:
12px;color:navy;' align='left'  nowrap='true'><select><option value = '" + va[c] +
"'>" + va[c] + "</option></select></td>\" + vbcrlf)");
    }
    txtstream.WriteLine("</tr>");
}
```

Vertical Using A Div

```
for(var c = 0;c < names.length;c++)
{
    txtstream.WriteLine("<tr><th          style='color:darkred;font-size:10px;font-
family:Cambria, serif;' align='left' nowrap>" + names[c] + "</th>");
    for(var d = 0;d < values.length;d++)
    {
       va = values[d];
       txtstream.WriteLine("<td              style='color:navy;font-size:10px;font-
family:Cambria, serif;' align='left' nowrap><div>" + va[c] + "</div></td>");
    }
    txtstream.WriteLine("</tr>")
}
```

Vertical Using A Link

```
for(var c = 0;c < names.length;c++)
{
    txtstream.WriteLine("<tr><th          style='color:darkred;font-size:10px;font-
family:Cambria, serif;' align='left' nowrap>" + names[c] + "</th>");
    for(var d = 0;d < values.length;d++)
    {
       va = values[d];
       txtstream.WriteLine("<td   style='font-family:Calibri,  Sans-Serif;font-size:
12px;color:navy;' align='left' nowrap='true'><a href='" + va[c] + "'>" + va[c] +
"</a></td>\" + vbcrlf)");
    }
    txtstream.WriteLine("</tr>");
}
```

Vertical Using A ListBox

```
for(var c = 0;c < names.length;c++)
{
    txtstream.WriteLine("<tr><th          style='color:darkred;font-size:10px;font-
family:Cambria, serif;' align='left' nowrap>" + names[c] + "</th>");
```

```
    for(var d = 0;d < values.length;d++)
    {
        va = values[d];
        txtstream.WriteLine("<td    style='font-family:Calibri,    Sans-Serif;font-size:
12px;color:navy;' align='left' nowrap='true'><select multiple><option value = '" +
va[c] + "'>" + va[c] + "</option></select></td>\" + vbcrlf)");
    }
    txtstream.WriteLine("</tr>");
}
```

Vertical Using A Span

```
for(var c = 0;c < names.length;c++)
{
    txtstream.WriteLine("<tr><th           style='color:darkred;font-size:10px;font-
family:Cambria, serif;' align='left' nowrap>" + names[c] + "</th>");
    for(var d = 0;d < values.length;d++)
    {
        va = values[d];
        txtstream.WriteLine("<td                style='color:navy;font-size:10px;font-
family:Cambria, serif;' align='left' nowrap><span>" + va[c] + "</span></td>");
    }
    txtstream.WriteLine("</tr>");
}
```

Vertical Using A Textarea

```
for(var c = 0;c < names.length;c++)
{
    txtstream.WriteLine("<tr><th           style='color:darkred;font-size:10px;font-
family:Cambria, serif;' align='left' nowrap>" + names[c] + "</th>");
    for(var d = 0;d < values.length;d++)
    {
        va = values[d];
        txtstream.WriteLine("<td                style='color:navy;font-size:10px;font-
family:Cambria,     serif;'    align='left'    nowrap><textarea>"    +    va[c]    +
"</textarea></td>");
    }
    txtstream.WriteLine("</tr>");
}
```

Vertical Using A TextBox

```
for(var c = 0;c < names.length;c++)
{
    txtstream.WriteLine("<tr><th        style='color:darkred;font-size:10px;font-
family:Cambria, serif;' align='left' nowrap>" + names[c] + "</th>");
    for(var d = 0;d < values.length;d++)
    {
      va = values[d];
      txtstream.WriteLine("<td        style='color:navy;font-size:10px;font-
family:Cambria, serif;' align='left' nowrap><input Type=text value=\"\" + va[c] +
\"\"></input></td>");
    }
    txtstream.WriteLine("</tr>");
}
```

End Code

```
    txtstream.WriteLine("</table>");
    txtstream.WriteLine("</body>");
    txtstream.WriteLine("</html>");
    txtstream.Close();
}
```

HTA TABLES

```
function Write_The_Code()
{

    var ws = new ActiveXObject("WScript.Shell");
    var filename = ws.CurrentDirectory + "\\Win32_Process.hta";
    var fso = new ActiveXObject("Scripting.FileSystemObject");
    var txtstream = fso.OpenTextFile(filename, 2, true, -2);
    txtstream.writeline("<html>");
    txtstream.WriteLine("<head>");
    txtstream.WriteLine("<HTA:APPLICATION ");
    txtstream.WriteLine(" ID = \"Win32_Process\" ");
    txtstream.WriteLine(" APPLICATIONNAME = \"Win32_Process\" ");
    txtstream.WriteLine(" SCROLL = \"Yes\" ");
    txtstream.WriteLine(" SINGLEINSTANCE = \"yes\" ");
    txtstream.WriteLine(" WINDOWSTATE = \"normal\">");
    txtstream.WriteLine("<title>Win32_Process</title>");
    txtstream.WriteLine("</head>");
    txtstream.WriteLine("<body>");
    txtstream.WriteLine("<table  boder=1 cellpadding=2 cellspacing=2>");
```

Horizontal No Additional Tags

```
for(var d = 0;d < values.length;d++)
{
   txtstream.WriteLine("<tr>");
   va = values[d];
   for(var c = 0;c < names.length;c++)
   {
       txtstream.WriteLine("<td                 style='color:navy;font-size:10px;font-
family:Cambria, serif;' align='left' nowrap>" + va[c] + "</td>");
   }
   txtstream.WriteLine("</tr>");
}
```

Horizontal Using A Button

```
for(var d = 0;d < values.length;d++)
{
   txtstream.WriteLine("<tr>");
   va = values[d];
   for(var c = 0;c < names.length;c++)
   {
       txtstream.WriteLine("<td                 style='color:navy;font-size:10px;font-
family:Cambria, serif;' align='left' nowrap><input Type= button value=\"\" + va[c] +
\"\"></input></td>");
   }
   txtstream.WriteLine("</tr>");
}
```

Horizontal Using A ComboBox

```
for(var d = 0;d < values.length;d++)

{

   txtstream.WriteLine("<tr>");
   va = values[d];
```

```
for(var c = 0;c < names.length;c++)
{
        txtstream.WriteLine("<td    style='font-family:Calibri,    Sans-Serif;font-size:
12px;color:navy;' align='left' nowrap='true'><select><option value = '" + va[c] +
"'>" + va[c] + "</option></select></td>\" + vbcrlf)");
        }
        txtstream.WriteLine("</tr>");
    }
```

Horizontal Using A Div

```
for(var d = 0;d < values.length;d++)
{
        txtstream.WriteLine("<tr>");
        va = values[d];
        for(var c = 0;c < names.length;c++)
        {

            txtstream.WriteLine("<td             style='color:navy;font-size:10px;font-
family:Cambria, serif;' align='left' nowrap><div>" + va[c] + "</div></td>");

    }
    txtstream.WriteLine("</tr>");
}
```

Horizontal Using A Link

```
for(var d = 0;d < values.length;d++)
{
    txtstream.WriteLine("<tr>");
    va = values[d];
    for(var c = 0;c < names.length;c++)
    {
        txtstream.WriteLine("<td    style='font-family:Calibri,    Sans-Serif;font-size:
12px;color:navy;' align='left' nowrap='true'><a href='" + va[c] + "'>" + va[c] +
"</a></td>\" + vbcrlf)");
    }
```

```
    txtstream.WriteLine("</tr>");
  }
```

Horizontal Using A ListBox

```
  for(var d = 0;d < values.length;d++

  {

    txtstream.WriteLine("<tr>");

    va = values[d];
    for(var c = 0;c < names.length;c++)
    {
        txtstream.WriteLine("<td   style='font-family:Calibri,   Sans-Serif;font-size:
12px;color:navy;' align='left' nowrap='true'><select multiple><option value = '" +
va[c] + "'>" + va[c] + "</option></select></td>\" + vbcrlf)");
    }
    txtstream.WriteLine("</tr>");
  }
```

Horizontal Using A Span

```
  for(var d = 0;d < values.length;d++

  {

    txtstream.WriteLine("<tr>");

    va = values[d];
    for(var c = 0;c < names.length;c++)
    {
        txtstream.WriteLine("<td                 style='color:navy;font-size:10px;font-
family:Cambria, serif;' align='left' nowrap><span>" + va[c] + "</span></td>");
    }
    txtstream.WriteLine("</tr>");
  }
```

Horizontal Using A Textarea

```
for(var d = 0;d < values.length;d++

{

    txtstream.WriteLine("<tr>");

    va = values[d];
    for(var c = 0;c < names.length;c++)
    {
        txtstream.WriteLine("<td                    style='color:navy;font-size:10px;font-
family:Cambria,    serif;'    align='left'    nowrap><textarea>"    +    va[c]    +
"</textarea></td>");
    }
    txtstream.WriteLine("</tr>");
}
```

Horizontal Using A TextBox

```
for(var d = 0;d < values.length;d++

{

    txtstream.WriteLine("<tr>");

    va = values[d];
    for(var c = 0;c < names.length;c++)
    {
        txtstream.WriteLine("<td                    style='color:navy;font-size:10px;font-
family:Cambria, serif;' align='left' nowrap><input Type=text value=\"\" + va[c] +
\"\"></input></td>");

    }
    txtstream.WriteLine("</tr>");
}
```

Vertical No Additional Controls

```
for(var c = 0;c < names.length;c++)
```

```
    {
        txtstream.WriteLine("<tr><th          style='color:darkred;font-size:10px;font-
family:Cambria, serif;' align='left' nowrap>" + names[c] + "</th>");
        for(var d = 0;d < values.length;d++)
        {
            va = values[d];
            txtstream.WriteLine("<td                 style='color:navy;font-size:10px;font-
family:Cambria, serif;' align='left' nowrap>" + va[c] + "</td>");
        }
        txtstream.WriteLine("</tr>");
    }
```

Vertical Using A Button

```
    for(var c = 0;c < names.length;c++)
    {
        txtstream.WriteLine("<tr><th          style='color:darkred;font-size:10px;font-
family:Cambria, serif;' align='left' nowrap>" + names[c] + "</th>");
        for(var d = 0;d < values.length;d++)
        {
            va = values[d];
            txtstream.WriteLine("<td                 style='color:navy;font-size:10px;font-
family:Cambria, serif;' align='left' nowrap><input Type= button value=\"\" + va[c] +
\"\"></input></td>");
        }
        txtstream.WriteLine("</tr>");
    }
```

Vertical Using A ComboBox

```
    for(var c = 0;c < names.length;c++)
    {
        txtstream.WriteLine("<tr><th          style='color:darkred;font-size:10px;font-
family:Cambria, serif;' align='left' nowrap>" + names[c] + "</th>");
        for(var d = 0;d < values.length;d++)
        {
            va = values[d];
```

```
        txtstream.WriteLine("<td    style='font-family:Calibri,   Sans-Serif;font-size:
12px;color:navy;' align='left' nowrap='true'><select><option value = '" + va[c] +
"'>" + va[c] + "</option></select></td>\" + vbcrlf)");
    }
    txtstream.WriteLine("</tr>");
  }
```

Vertical Using A Div

```
  for(var c = 0;c < names.length;c++)
  {
      txtstream.WriteLine("<tr><th         style='color:darkred;font-size:10px;font-
family:Cambria, serif;' align='left' nowrap>" + names[c] + "</th>");
      for(var d = 0;d < values.length;d++)
      {
        va = values[d];
      , txtstream.WriteLine("<td           style='color:navy;font-size:10px;font-
family:Cambria, serif;' align='left' nowrap><div>" + va[c] + "</div></td>");
      }
      txtstream.WriteLine("</tr>")
  }
```

Vertical Using A Link

```
  for(var c = 0;c < names.length;c++)
  {
      txtstream.WriteLine("<tr><th         style='color:darkred;font-size:10px;font-
family:Cambria, serif;' align='left' nowrap>" + names[c] + "</th>");
      for(var d = 0;d < values.length;d++)
      {
        va = values[d];
        txtstream.WriteLine("<td    style='font-family:Calibri,   Sans-Serif;font-size:
12px;color:navy;' align='left' nowrap='true'><a href='" + va[c] + "'>" + va[c] +
"</a></td>\" + vbcrlf)");
      }
      txtstream.WriteLine("</tr>");
  }
```

Vertical Using A ListBox

```
for(var c = 0;c < names.length;c++)
{
    txtstream.WriteLine("<tr><th          style='color:darkred;font-size:10px;font-
family:Cambria, serif;' align='left' nowrap>" + names[c] + "</th>");
    for(var d = 0;d < values.length;d++)
    {
       va = values[d];
       txtstream.WriteLine("<td   style='font-family:Calibri,   Sans-Serif;font-size:
12px;color:navy;' align='left' nowrap='true'><select multiple><option value = '" +
va[c] + "'>" + va[c] + "</option></select></td>\" + vbcrlf)");
    }
    txtstream.WriteLine("</tr>");
}
```

Vertical Using A Span

```
for(var c = 0;c < names.length;c++)
{
    txtstream.WriteLine("<tr><th          style='color:darkred;font-size:10px;font-
family:Cambria, serif;' align='left' nowrap>" + names[c] + "</th>");
    for(var d = 0;d < values.length;d++)
    {
       va = values[d];
       txtstream.WriteLine("<td            style='color:navy;font-size:10px;font-
family:Cambria, serif;' align='left' nowrap><span>" + va[c] + "</span></td>");
    }
    txtstream.WriteLine("</tr>");
}
```

Vertical Using A Textarea

```
for(var c = 0;c < names.length;c++)
{
    txtstream.WriteLine("<tr><th          style='color:darkred;font-size:10px;font-
family:Cambria, serif;' align='left' nowrap>" + names[c] + "</th>");
    for(var d = 0;d < values.length;d++)
    {
       va = values[d];
```

```
        txtstream.WriteLine("<td                    style='color:navy;font-size:10px;font-
family:Cambria,    serif;'    align='left'    nowrap><textarea>"    +    va[c]    +
"</textarea></td>");
    }
    txtstream.WriteLine("</tr>");
  }
```

Vertical Using A TextBox

```
  for(var c = 0;c < names.length;c++)
  {
      txtstream.WriteLine("<tr><th              style='color:darkred;font-size:10px;font-
family:Cambria, serif;' align='left' nowrap>" + names[c] + "</th>");
      for(var d = 0;d < values.length;d++)
      {
        va = values[d];
        txtstream.WriteLine("<td                   style='color:navy;font-size:10px;font-
family:Cambria, serif;' align='left' nowrap><input Type=text value=\"\" + va[c] +
\"\"></input></td>");
      }
      txtstream.WriteLine("</tr>");
  }
```

End Code

```
  txtstream.WriteLine("</table>");
  txtstream.WriteLine("</body>");
  txtstream.WriteLine("</html>");
  txtstream.Close();
}
```

HTML REPORTS

Begin Code

```
function Write_The_Code()
{

    var ws = new ActiveXObject("WScript.Shell");
    var filename = ws.CurrentDirectory + "\\Win32_Process.hta";
    var fso = new ActiveXObject("Scripting.FileSystemObject");
    var txtstream = fso.OpenTextFile(filename, 2, true, -2);
    txtstream.writeline("<html>");
    txtstream.WriteLine("<head>");
    txtstream.WriteLine("<title>Win32_Process</title>");
    txtstream.WriteLine("</head>");
    txtstream.WriteLine("<body>");
    txtstream.WriteLine("<table  boder=0 cellpadding=2 cellspacing=2>");
```

Horizontal No Additional Tags

```
    for(var d = 0;d < values.length;d++)
    {
        txtstream.WriteLine("<tr>");
        va = values[d];
```

```
  for(var c = 0;c < names.length;c++)
  {
      txtstream.WriteLine("<td            style='color:navy;font-size:10px;font-
family:Cambria, serif;' align='left' nowrap>" + va[c] + "</td>");
  }
  txtstream.WriteLine("</tr>");
}
```

Horizontal Using A Button

```
for(var d = 0;d < values.length;d++)
{
    txtstream.WriteLine("<tr>");
    va = values[d];
    for(var c = 0;c < names.length;c++)
    {
        txtstream.WriteLine("<td            style='color:navy;font-size:10px;font-
family:Cambria, serif;' align='left' nowrap><input Type= button value=\"\" + va[c] +
\"\"></input></td>");
    }
    txtstream.WriteLine("</tr>");
}
```

Horizontal Using A ComboBox

```
for(var d = 0;d < values.length;d++)
{

    txtstream.WriteLine("<tr>");
    va = values[d];
    for(var c = 0;c < names.length;c++)
    {
        txtstream.WriteLine("<td    style='font-family:Calibri,   Sans-Serif;font-size:
12px;color:navy;' align='left' nowrap='true'><select><option value = '" + va[c] +
"'>" + va[c] + "</option></select></td>\" + vbcrlf)");
    }
    txtstream.WriteLine("</tr>");
```

```
}
```

Horizontal Using A Div

```
for(var d = 0;d < values.length;d++)
{
        txtstream.WriteLine("<tr>");
        va = values[d];
        for(var c = 0;c < names.length;c++)
        {

            txtstream.WriteLine("<td          style='color:navy;font-size:10px;font-
family:Cambria, serif;' align='left' nowrap><div>" + va[c] + "</div></td>");

        }
    txtstream.WriteLine("</tr>");
}
```

Horizontal Using A Link

```
for(var d = 0;d < values.length;d++)
{
    txtstream.WriteLine("<tr>");
    va = values[d];
    for(var c = 0;c < names.length;c++)
    {
        txtstream.WriteLine("<td   style='font-family:Calibri,   Sans-Serif;font-size:
12px;color:navy;' align='left' nowrap='true'><a href='" + va[c] + "'>" + va[c] +
"</a></td>\" + vbcrlf)");
    }
    txtstream.WriteLine("</tr>");
}
```

Horizontal Using A ListBox

```
for(var d = 0;d < values.length;d++

    {
```

```
    txtstream.WriteLine("<tr>");

    va = values[d];
    for(var c = 0;c < names.length;c++)
    {
        txtstream.WriteLine("<td    style='font-family:Calibri,    Sans-Serif;font-size:
12px;color:navy;' align='left' nowrap='true'><select multiple><option value = '" +
va[c] + "'>" + va[c] + "</option></select></td>\" + vbcrlf)");
    }
    txtstream.WriteLine("</tr>");
  }
```

Horizontal Using A Span

```
  for(var d = 0;d < values.length;d++

  {

    txtstream.WriteLine("<tr>");

    va = values[d];
    for(var c = 0;c < names.length;c++)
    {
        txtstream.WriteLine("<td                    style='color:navy;font-size:10px;font-
family:Cambria, serif;' align='left' nowrap><span>" + va[c] + "</span></td>");
    }
    txtstream.WriteLine("</tr>");
  }
```

Horizontal Using A Textarea

```
  for(var d = 0;d < values.length;d++

  {

    txtstream.WriteLine("<tr>");

    va = values[d];
    for(var c = 0;c < names.length;c++)
```

```
    {
        txtstream.WriteLine("<td          style='color:navy;font-size:10px;font-
family:Cambria,    serif;'    align='left'    nowrap><textarea>"    +    va[c]    +
"</textarea></td>");
    }
    txtstream.WriteLine("</tr>");
  }
```

Horizontal Using A TextBox

```
  for(var d = 0;d < values.length;d++

  {

    txtstream.WriteLine("<tr>");

    va = values[d];
    for(var c = 0;c < names.length;c++)
    {
        txtstream.WriteLine("<td          style='color:navy;font-size:10px;font-
family:Cambria, serif;' align='left' nowrap><input Type=text value=\"\" + va[c] +
\"\"></input></td>");

    }
    txtstream.WriteLine("</tr>");
  }
```

Vertical No Additional Controls

```
  for(var c = 0;c < names.length;c++)
  {
    txtstream.WriteLine("<tr><th          style='color:darkred;font-size:10px;font-
family:Cambria, serif;' align='left' nowrap>" + names[c] + "</th>");
    for(var d = 0;d < values.length;d++)
    {
      va = values[d];
      txtstream.WriteLine("<td          style='color:navy;font-size:10px;font-
family:Cambria, serif;' align='left' nowrap>" + va[c] + "</td>");
```

```
        }
        txtstream.WriteLine("</tr>");
    }
```

Vertical Using A Button

```
    for(var c = 0;c < names.length;c++)
    {
        txtstream.WriteLine("<tr><th          style='color:darkred;font-size:10px;font-
    family:Cambria, serif;' align='left' nowrap>" + names[c] + "</th>");
        for(var d = 0;d < values.length;d++)
        {
            va = values[d];
            txtstream.WriteLine("<td          style='color:navy;font-size:10px;font-
        family:Cambria, serif;' align='left' nowrap><input Type= button value=\"\" + va[c] +
        \"\"></input></td>");
        }
        txtstream.WriteLine("</tr>");
    }
```

Vertical Using A ComboBox

```
    for(var c = 0;c < names.length;c++)
    {
        txtstream.WriteLine("<tr><th          style='color:darkred;font-size:10px;font-
    family:Cambria, serif;' align='left' nowrap>" + names[c] + "</th>");
        for(var d = 0;d < values.length;d++)
        {
            va = values[d];
            txtstream.WriteLine("<td    style='font-family:Calibri,    Sans-Serif;font-size:
        12px;color:navy;' align='left' nowrap='true'><select><option value = '" + va[c] +
        "'>" + va[c] + "</option></select></td>\" + vbcrlf)");
        }
        txtstream.WriteLine("</tr>");
    }
```

Vertical Using A Div

```
for(var c = 0;c < names.length;c++)
{
    txtstream.WriteLine("<tr><th          style='color:darkred;font-size:10px;font-
family:Cambria, serif;' align='left' nowrap>" + names[c] + "</th>");
    for(var d = 0;d < values.length;d++)
    {
      va = values[d];
      txtstream.WriteLine("<td          style='color:navy;font-size:10px;font-
family:Cambria, serif;' align='left' nowrap><div>" + va[c] + "</div></td>");
    }
    txtstream.WriteLine("</tr>")
}
```

Vertical Using A Link

```
for(var c = 0;c < names.length;c++)
{
    txtstream.WriteLine("<tr><th          style='color:darkred;font-size:10px;font-
family:Cambria, serif;' align='left' nowrap>" + names[c] + "</th>");
    for(var d = 0;d < values.length;d++)
    {
      va = values[d];
      txtstream.WriteLine("<td   style='font-family:Calibri,   Sans-Serif;font-size:
12px;color:navy;' align='left' nowrap='true'><a href='" + va[c] + "'>" + va[c] +
"</a></td>\" + vbcrlf)");
    }
    txtstream.WriteLine("</tr>");
}
```

Vertical Using A ListBox

```
for(var c = 0;c < names.length;c++)
{
    txtstream.WriteLine("<tr><th          style='color:darkred;font-size:10px;font-
family:Cambria, serif;' align='left' nowrap>" + names[c] + "</th>");
    for(var d = 0;d < values.length;d++)
```

```
    {
      va = values[d];
      txtstream.WriteLine("<td    style='font-family:Calibri,    Sans-Serif;font-size:
12px;color:navy;' align='left' nowrap='true'><select multiple><option value = '" +
va[c] + "'>" + va[c] + "</option></select></td>\" + vbcrlf)");
    }
    txtstream.WriteLine("</tr>");
  }
```

Vertical Using A Span

```
  for(var c = 0;c < names.length;c++)
  {
    txtstream.WriteLine("<tr><th            style='color:darkred;font-size:10px;font-
family:Cambria, serif;' align='left' nowrap>" + names[c] + "</th>");
    for(var d = 0;d < values.length;d++)
    {
      va = values[d];
      txtstream.WriteLine("<td             style='color:navy;font-size:10px;font-
family:Cambria, serif;' align='left' nowrap><span>" + va[c] + "</span></td>");
    }
    txtstream.WriteLine("</tr>");
  }
```

Vertical Using A Textarea

```
  for(var c = 0;c < names.length;c++)
  {
    txtstream.WriteLine("<tr><th            style='color:darkred;font-size:10px;font-
family:Cambria, serif;' align='left' nowrap>" + names[c] + "</th>");
    for(var d = 0;d < values.length;d++)
    {
      va = values[d];
      txtstream.WriteLine("<td             style='color:navy;font-size:10px;font-
family:Cambria,    serif;'    align='left'    nowrap><textarea>"    +    va[c]    +
"</textarea></td>");
    }
    txtstream.WriteLine("</tr>");
  }
```

Vertical Using A TextBox

```
for(var c = 0;c < names.length;c++)
{
    txtstream.WriteLine("<tr><th          style='color:darkred;font-size:10px;font-
family:Cambria, serif;' align='left' nowrap>" + names[c] + "</th>");
    for(var d = 0;d < values.length;d++)
    {
      va = values[d];
      txtstream.WriteLine("<td            style='color:navy;font-size:10px;font-
family:Cambria, serif;' align='left' nowrap><input Type=text value=\"\" + va[c] +
\"\"></input></td>");
    }
    txtstream.WriteLine("</tr>");
}
```

End Code

```
    txtstream.WriteLine("</table>");
    txtstream.WriteLine("</body>");
    txtstream.WriteLine("</html>");
    txtstream.Close();
}
```

HTML TABLES

Begin Code

```
function Write_The_Code()
{

    var ws = new ActiveXObject("WScript.Shell");
    var filename = ws.CurrentDirectory + "\\Win32_Process.hta";
    var fso = new ActiveXObject("Scripting.FileSystemObject");
    var txtstream = fso.OpenTextFile(filename, 2, true, -2);
    txtstream.writeline("<html>");
    txtstream.WriteLine("<head>");
    txtstream.WriteLine("<title>Win32_Process</title>");
    txtstream.WriteLine("</head>");
    txtstream.WriteLine("<body>");
    txtstream.WriteLine("<table  boder=1 cellpadding=2 cellspacing=2>");
```

Horizontal No Additional Tags

```
    for(var d = 0;d < values.length;d++)
    {
      txtstream.WriteLine("<tr>");
      va = values[d];
      for(var c = 0;c < names.length;c++)
      {
```

```
      txtstream.WriteLine("<td                    style='color:navy;font-size:10px;font-
family:Cambria, serif;' align='left' nowrap>" + va[c] + "</td>");
    }
    txtstream.WriteLine("</tr>");
  }
```

Horizontal Using A Button

```
  for(var d = 0;d < values.length;d++)
  {
    txtstream.WriteLine("<tr>");
    va = values[d];
    for(var c = 0;c < names.length;c++)
    {
      txtstream.WriteLine("<td                    style='color:navy;font-size:10px;font-
family:Cambria, serif;' align='left' nowrap><input Type= button value=\"\" + va[c] +
\"\"></input></td>");
    }
    txtstream.WriteLine("</tr>");
  }
```

Horizontal Using A ComboBox

```
  for(var d = 0;d < values.length;d++)

  {

    txtstream.WriteLine("<tr>");
    va = values[d];
    for(var c = 0;c < names.length;c++)
    {
      txtstream.WriteLine("<td   style='font-family:Calibri,   Sans-Serif;font-size:
12px;color:navy;' align='left' nowrap='true'><select><option value = '" + va[c] +
"'>" + va[c] + "</option></select></td>\" + vbcrlf)");
    }
    txtstream.WriteLine("</tr>");
  }
```

Horizontal Using A Div

```
for(var d = 0;d < values.length;d++)
{
        txtstream.WriteLine("<tr>");
        va = values[d];
        for(var c = 0;c < names.length;c++)
        {

                txtstream.WriteLine("<td          style='color:navy;font-size:10px;font-
family:Cambria, serif;' align='left' nowrap><div>" + va[c] + "</div></td>");

        }
        txtstream.WriteLine("</tr>");
}
```

Horizontal Using A Link

```
for(var d = 0;d < values.length;d++)
{
    txtstream.WriteLine("<tr>");
    va = values[d];
    for(var c = 0;c < names.length;c++)
    {
        txtstream.WriteLine("<td    style='font-family:Calibri,   Sans-Serif;font-size:
12px;color:navy;' align='left' nowrap='true'><a href='" + va[c] + "'>" + va[c] +
"</a></td>\" + vbcrlf)");
    }
    txtstream.WriteLine("</tr>");
}
```

Horizontal Using A ListBox

```
for(var d = 0;d < values.length;d++

{

    txtstream.WriteLine("<tr>");
```

```
        va = values[d];
        for(var c = 0;c < names.length;c++)
        {
            txtstream.WriteLine("<td    style='font-family:Calibri,    Sans-Serif;font-size:
12px;color:navy;' align='left' nowrap='true'><select multiple><option value = '" +
va[c] + "'>" + va[c] + "</option></select></td>\" + vbcrlf)");
        }
        txtstream.WriteLine("</tr>");
    }
```

Horizontal Using A Span

```
    for(var d = 0;d < values.length;d++

    {

        txtstream.WriteLine("<tr>");

        va = values[d];
        for(var c = 0;c < names.length;c++)
        {
            txtstream.WriteLine("<td                    style='color:navy;font-size:10px;font-
family:Cambria, serif;' align='left' nowrap><span>" + va[c] + "</span></td>");
        }
        txtstream.WriteLine("</tr>");
    }
```

Horizontal Using A Textarea

```
    for(var d = 0;d < values.length;d++

    {

        txtstream.WriteLine("<tr>");

        va = values[d];
        for(var c = 0;c < names.length;c++)
        {
```

```
        txtstream.WriteLine("<td                    style='color:navy;font-size:10px;font-
family:Cambria,    serif;'    align='left'    nowrap><textarea>"    +    va[c]    +
"</textarea></td>");
    }
    txtstream.WriteLine("</tr>");
  }
```

Horizontal Using A TextBox

```
  for(var d = 0;d < values.length;d++

  {

    txtstream.WriteLine("<tr>");

    va = values[d];
    for(var c = 0;c < names.length;c++)
    {
        txtstream.WriteLine("<td                    style='color:navy;font-size:10px;font-
family:Cambria, serif;' align='left' nowrap><input Type=text value=\"\" + va[c] +
\"\"></input></td>");

    }
    txtstream.WriteLine("</tr>");
  }
```

Vertical No Additional Controls

```
  for(var c = 0;c < names.length;c++)
  {
      txtstream.WriteLine("<tr><th              style='color:darkred;font-size:10px;font-
family:Cambria, serif;' align='left' nowrap>" + names[c] + "</th>");
    for(var d = 0;d < values.length;d++)
    {
      va = values[d];
      txtstream.WriteLine("<td                  style='color:navy;font-size:10px;font-
family:Cambria, serif;' align='left' nowrap>" + va[c] + "</td>");
    }
```

```
    txtstream.WriteLine("</tr>");
  }
```

Vertical Using A Button

```
  for(var c = 0;c < names.length;c++)
  {
    txtstream.WriteLine("<tr><th          style='color:darkred;font-size:10px;font-
family:Cambria, serif;' align='left' nowrap>" + names[c] + "</th>");
    for(var d = 0;d < values.length;d++)
    {
      va = values[d];
      txtstream.WriteLine("<td            style='color:navy;font-size:10px;font-
family:Cambria, serif;' align='left' nowrap><input Type= button value=\"\" + va[c] +
\"\"></input></td>");
    }
    txtstream.WriteLine("</tr>");
  }
```

Vertical Using A ComboBox

```
  for(var c = 0;c < names.length;c++)
  {
    txtstream.WriteLine("<tr><th          style='color:darkred;font-size:10px;font-
family:Cambria, serif;' align='left' nowrap>" + names[c] + "</th>");
    for(var d = 0;d < values.length;d++)
    {
      va = values[d];
      txtstream.WriteLine("<td   style='font-family:Calibri,   Sans-Serif;font-size:
12px;color:navy;' align='left' nowrap='true'><select><option value = '" + va[c] +
"'>" + va[c] + "</option></select></td>\" + vbcrlf)");
    }
    txtstream.WriteLine("</tr>");
  }
```

Vertical Using A Div

```
for(var c = 0;c < names.length;c++)
{
    txtstream.WriteLine("<tr><th          style='color:darkred;font-size:10px;font-
family:Cambria, serif;' align='left' nowrap>" + names[c] + "</th>");
    for(var d = 0;d < values.length;d++)
    {
      va = values[d];
        txtstream.WriteLine("<td          style='color:navy;font-size:10px;font-
family:Cambria, serif;' align='left' nowrap><div>" + va[c] + "</div></td>");
    }
    txtstream.WriteLine("</tr>")
}
```

Vertical Using A Link

```
for(var c = 0;c < names.length;c++)
{
    txtstream.WriteLine("<tr><th          style='color:darkred;font-size:10px;font-
family:Cambria, serif;' align='left' nowrap>" + names[c] + "</th>");
    for(var d = 0;d < values.length;d++)
    {
      va = values[d];
        txtstream.WriteLine("<td   style='font-family:Calibri,   Sans-Serif;font-size:
12px;color:navy;' align='left' nowrap='true'><a href='" + va[c] + "'>" + va[c] +
"</a></td>\" + vbcrlf)");
    }
    txtstream.WriteLine("</tr>");
}
```

Vertical Using A ListBox

```
for(var c = 0;c < names.length;c++)
{
    txtstream.WriteLine("<tr><th          style='color:darkred;font-size:10px;font-
family:Cambria, serif;' align='left' nowrap>" + names[c] + "</th>");
    for(var d = 0;d < values.length;d++)
    {
      va = values[d];
```

```
        txtstream.WriteLine("<td    style='font-family:Calibri,    Sans-Serif;font-size:
12px;color:navy;' align='left' nowrap='true'><select multiple><option value = '" +
va[c] + "'>" + va[c] + "</option></select></td>\" + vbcrlf)");
    }
    txtstream.WriteLine("</tr>");
}
```

Vertical Using A Span

```
for(var c = 0;c < names.length;c++)
{
    txtstream.WriteLine("<tr><th          style='color:darkred;font-size:10px;font-
family:Cambria, serif;' align='left' nowrap>" + names[c] + "</th>");
    for(var d = 0;d < values.length;d++)
    {
      va = values[d];
      txtstream.WriteLine("<td              style='color:navy;font-size:10px;font-
family:Cambria, serif;' align='left' nowrap><span>" + va[c] + "</span></td>");
    }
    txtstream.WriteLine("</tr>");
}
```

Vertical Using A Textarea

```
for(var c = 0;c < names.length;c++)
{
    txtstream.WriteLine("<tr><th          style='color:darkred;font-size:10px;font-
family:Cambria, serif;' align='left' nowrap>" + names[c] + "</th>");
    for(var d = 0;d < values.length;d++)
    {
      va = values[d];
      txtstream.WriteLine("<td              style='color:navy;font-size:10px;font-
family:Cambria,    serif;'    align='left'    nowrap><textarea>"    +    va[c]    +
"</textarea></td>");
    }
    txtstream.WriteLine("</tr>");
}
```

Vertical Using A TextBox

```
for(var c = 0;c < names.length;c++)
{
    txtstream.WriteLine("<tr><th          style='color:darkred;font-size:10px;font-
family:Cambria, serif;' align='left' nowrap>" + names[c] + "</th>");
    for(var d = 0;d < values.length;d++)
    {
        va = values[d];
        txtstream.WriteLine("<td          style='color:navy;font-size:10px;font-
family:Cambria, serif;' align='left' nowrap><input Type=text value=\"\" + va[c] +
\"\"></input></td>");
    }
    txtstream.WriteLine("</tr>");
}
```

End Code

```
    txtstream.WriteLine("</table>");
    txtstream.WriteLine("</body>");
    txtstream.WriteLine("</html>");
    txtstream.Close();
}
```

Stylesheets

Decorating your web pages

BELOW ARE SOME STYLESHEETS I COOKED UP THAT I LIKE AND THINK YOU MIGHT TOO. Don't worry I won't be offended if you take and modify to your hearts delight. Please do!

NONE

```
txtstream.WriteLine('<style type='text/css'>")

txtstream.WriteLine("   th")

txtstream.WriteLine("   begin")

txtstream.WriteLine("   COLOR: darkred;")

txtstream.WriteLine("   BACKGROUND-COLOR: white;")

txtstream.WriteLine("   FONT-FAMILY:font-family: Cambria, serif;")

txtstream.WriteLine("   FONT-SIZE: 12px;")

txtstream.WriteLine("   text-align: left;")

txtstream.WriteLine("   white-Space: nowrap;")

txtstream.WriteLine("   end;")

txtstream.WriteLine("   td")

txtstream.WriteLine("   begin")

txtstream.WriteLine("   COLOR: navy;")

txtstream.WriteLine("   BACKGROUND-COLOR: white;")
```

```
txtstream.WriteLine("    FONT-FAMILY: font-family: Cambria, serif;")
txtstream.WriteLine("    FONT-SIZE: 12px;")
txtstream.WriteLine("    text-align: left;")
txtstream.WriteLine("    white-Space: nowrap;")
txtstream.WriteLine("    end;")
txtstream.WriteLine("    </style>');
```

BLACK AND WHITE TEXT

```
txtstream.WriteLine("    <style type='text/css'>');
txtstream.WriteLine("    th")
txtstream.WriteLine("    begin")
txtstream.WriteLine("        COLOR: white;")
txtstream.WriteLine("        BACKGROUND-COLOR: black;")
txtstream.WriteLine("        FONT-FAMILY:font-family: Cambria, serif;")
txtstream.WriteLine("        FONT-SIZE: 12px;")
txtstream.WriteLine("        text-align: left;")
txtstream.WriteLine("        white-Space: nowrap;")
txtstream.WriteLine("    end;")
txtstream.WriteLine("    td")
txtstream.WriteLine("    begin")
txtstream.WriteLine("        COLOR: white;")
txtstream.WriteLine("        BACKGROUND-COLOR: black;")
txtstream.WriteLine("        FONT-FAMILY: font-family: Cambria, serif;")
txtstream.WriteLine("        FONT-SIZE: 12px;")
txtstream.WriteLine("        text-align: left;")
```

```
txtstream.WriteLine("      white-Space: nowrap;")
txtstream.WriteLine("   end;")
txtstream.WriteLine("   div")
txtstream.WriteLine("   begin")
txtstream.WriteLine("      COLOR: white;")
txtstream.WriteLine("      BACKGROUND-COLOR: black;")
txtstream.WriteLine("      FONT-FAMILY: font-family: Cambria, serif;")
txtstream.WriteLine("      FONT-SIZE: 10px;")
txtstream.WriteLine("      text-align: left;")
txtstream.WriteLine("      white-Space: nowrap;")
txtstream.WriteLine("   end;")
txtstream.WriteLine("   span")
txtstream.WriteLine("   begin")
txtstream.WriteLine("      COLOR: white;")
txtstream.WriteLine("      BACKGROUND-COLOR: black;")
txtstream.WriteLine("      FONT-FAMILY: font-family: Cambria, serif;")
txtstream.WriteLine("      FONT-SIZE: 10px;")
txtstream.WriteLine("      text-align: left;")
txtstream.WriteLine("      white-Space: nowrap;")
txtstream.WriteLine("      display:inline-block;")
txtstream.WriteLine("      width: 100%;")
txtstream.WriteLine("   end;")
txtstream.WriteLine("   textarea")
txtstream.WriteLine("   begin")
txtstream.WriteLine("      COLOR: white;")
txtstream.WriteLine("      BACKGROUND-COLOR: black;")
txtstream.WriteLine("      FONT-FAMILY: font-family: Cambria, serif;")
```

```
txtstream.WriteLine("     FONT-SIZE: 10px;")

txtstream.WriteLine("     text-align: left;")

txtstream.WriteLine("     white-Space: nowrap;")

txtstream.WriteLine("     width: 100%;")

txtstream.WriteLine("   end;")

txtstream.WriteLine("   select")

txtstream.WriteLine("   begin")

txtstream.WriteLine("     COLOR: white;")

txtstream.WriteLine("     BACKGROUND-COLOR: black;")

txtstream.WriteLine("     FONT-FAMILY: font-family: Cambria, serif;")

txtstream.WriteLine("     FONT-SIZE: 10px;")

txtstream.WriteLine("     text-align: left;")

txtstream.WriteLine("     white-Space: nowrap;")

txtstream.WriteLine("     width: 100%;")

txtstream.WriteLine("   end;")

txtstream.WriteLine("   input")

txtstream.WriteLine("   begin")

txtstream.WriteLine("     COLOR: white;")

txtstream.WriteLine("     BACKGROUND-COLOR: black;")

txtstream.WriteLine("     FONT-FAMILY: font-family: Cambria, serif;")

txtstream.WriteLine("     FONT-SIZE: 12px;")

txtstream.WriteLine("     text-align: left;")

txtstream.WriteLine("     display:table-cell;")

txtstream.WriteLine("     white-Space: nowrap;")

txtstream.WriteLine("   end;")

txtstream.WriteLine("   h1 begin")

txtstream.WriteLine("   color: antiquewhite;")
```

```
txtstream.WriteLine("   text-shadow: 1px 1px 1px black;")

txtstream.WriteLine("   padding: 3px;")

txtstream.WriteLine("   text-align: center;")

txtstream.WriteLine("   box-shadow: inset 2px 2px 5px rgba(0,0,0,0.5);, inset -2px
-2px 5px rgba(255,255,255,0.5);;")

txtstream.WriteLine("   end;")

txtstream.WriteLine("   </style>');
```

COLORED TEXT

```
txtstream.WriteLine("   <style type='text/css'>');

txtstream.WriteLine("   th")

txtstream.WriteLine("   begin")

txtstream.WriteLine("     COLOR: darkred;")

txtstream.WriteLine("     BACKGROUND-COLOR: #eeeeee;")

txtstream.WriteLine("     FONT-FAMILY:font-family: Cambria, serif;")

txtstream.WriteLine("     FONT-SIZE: 12px;")

txtstream.WriteLine("     text-align: left;")

txtstream.WriteLine("     white-Space: nowrap;")

txtstream.WriteLine("   end;")

txtstream.WriteLine("   td")

txtstream.WriteLine("   begin")

txtstream.WriteLine("     COLOR: navy;")

txtstream.WriteLine("     BACKGROUND-COLOR: #eeeeee;")

txtstream.WriteLine("     FONT-FAMILY: font-family: Cambria, serif;")

txtstream.WriteLine("     FONT-SIZE: 12px;")

txtstream.WriteLine("     text-align: left;")
```

```
txtstream.WriteLine("        white-Space: nowrap;")
txtstream.WriteLine("    end;")
txtstream.WriteLine("    div")
txtstream.WriteLine("    begin")
txtstream.WriteLine("        COLOR: white;")
txtstream.WriteLine("        BACKGROUND-COLOR: navy;")
txtstream.WriteLine("        FONT-FAMILY: font-family: Cambria, serif;")
txtstream.WriteLine("        FONT-SIZE: 10px;")
txtstream.WriteLine("        text-align: left;")
txtstream.WriteLine("        white-Space: nowrap;")
txtstream.WriteLine("    end;")
txtstream.WriteLine("    span")
txtstream.WriteLine("    begin")
txtstream.WriteLine("        COLOR: white;")
txtstream.WriteLine("        BACKGROUND-COLOR: navy;")
txtstream.WriteLine("        FONT-FAMILY: font-family: Cambria, serif;")
txtstream.WriteLine("        FONT-SIZE: 10px;")
txtstream.WriteLine("        text-align: left;")
txtstream.WriteLine("        white-Space: nowrap;")
txtstream.WriteLine("        display:inline-block;")
txtstream.WriteLine("        width: 100%;")
txtstream.WriteLine("    end;")
txtstream.WriteLine("    textarea")
txtstream.WriteLine("    begin")
txtstream.WriteLine("        COLOR: white;")
txtstream.WriteLine("        BACKGROUND-COLOR: navy;")
txtstream.WriteLine("        FONT-FAMILY: font-family: Cambria, serif;")
```

```
txtstream.WriteLine("        FONT-SIZE: 10px;")
txtstream.WriteLine("        text-align: left;")
txtstream.WriteLine("        white-Space: nowrap;")
txtstream.WriteLine("        width: 100%;")
txtstream.WriteLine("    end;")
txtstream.WriteLine("    select")
txtstream.WriteLine("    begin")
txtstream.WriteLine("        COLOR: white;")
txtstream.WriteLine("        BACKGROUND-COLOR: navy;")
txtstream.WriteLine("        FONT-FAMILY: font-family: Cambria, scrif;")
txtstream.WriteLine("        FONT-SIZE: 10px;")
txtstream.WriteLine("        text-align: left;")
txtstream.WriteLine("        white-Space: nowrap;")
txtstream.WriteLine("        width: 100%;")
txtstream.WriteLine("    end;")
txtstream.WriteLine("    input")
txtstream.WriteLine("    begin")
txtstream.WriteLine("        COLOR: white;")
txtstream.WriteLine("        BACKGROUND-COLOR: navy;")
txtstream.WriteLine("        FONT-FAMILY: font-family: Cambria, serif;")
txtstream.WriteLine("        FONT-SIZE: 12px;")
txtstream.WriteLine("        text-align: left;")
txtstream.WriteLine("        display:table-cell;")
txtstream.WriteLine("        white-Space: nowrap;")
txtstream.WriteLine("    end;")
txtstream.WriteLine("    h1 begin")
txtstream.WriteLine("        color: antiquewhite;")
```

txtstream.WriteLine(" text-shadow: 1px 1px 1px black;")

txtstream.WriteLine(" padding: 3px;")

txtstream.WriteLine(" text-align: center;")

txtstream.WriteLine(" box-shadow: inset 2px 2px 5px rgba(0,0,0,0.5);, inset -2px -2px 5px rgba(255,255,255,0.5);;")

txtstream.WriteLine(" end;")

txtstream.WriteLine(" </style>');

OSCILLATING ROW COLORS

txtstream.WriteLine(" <style>');

txtstream.WriteLine(" th")

txtstream.WriteLine(" begin")

txtstream.WriteLine(" COLOR: white;")

txtstream.WriteLine(" BACKGROUND-COLOR: navy;")

txtstream.WriteLine(" FONT-FAMILY:font-family: Cambria, serif;")

txtstream.WriteLine(" FONT-SIZE: 12px;")

txtstream.WriteLine(" text-align: left;")

txtstream.WriteLine(" white-Space: nowrap;")

txtstream.WriteLine(" end;")

txtstream.WriteLine(" td")

txtstream.WriteLine(" begin")

txtstream.WriteLine(" COLOR: navy;")

txtstream.WriteLine(" FONT-FAMILY: font-family: Cambria, serif;")

txtstream.WriteLine(" FONT-SIZE: 12px;")

```
txtstream.WriteLine("      text-align: left;")
txtstream.WriteLine("      white-Space: nowrap;")
txtstream.WriteLine("   end;")
txtstream.WriteLine("   div")
txtstream.WriteLine("   begin")
txtstream.WriteLine("      COLOR: navy;")
txtstream.WriteLine("      FONT-FAMILY: font-family: Cambria, serif;")
txtstream.WriteLine("      FONT-SIZE: 12px;")
txtstream.WriteLine("      text-align: left;")
txtstream.WriteLine("      white-Space: nowrap;")
txtstream.WriteLine("   end;")
txtstream.WriteLine("   span")
txtstream.WriteLine("   begin")
txtstream.WriteLine("      COLOR: navy;")
txtstream.WriteLine("      FONT-FAMILY: font-family: Cambria, serif;")
txtstream.WriteLine("      FONT-SIZE: 12px;")
txtstream.WriteLine("      text-align: left;")
txtstream.WriteLine("      white-Space: nowrap;")
txtstream.WriteLine("      width: 100%;")
txtstream.WriteLine("   end;")
txtstream.WriteLine("   textarea")
txtstream.WriteLine("   begin")
txtstream.WriteLine("      COLOR: navy;")
txtstream.WriteLine("      FONT-FAMILY: font-family: Cambria, serif;")
txtstream.WriteLine("      FONT-SIZE: 12px;")
txtstream.WriteLine("      text-align: left;")
txtstream.WriteLine("      white-Space: nowrap;")
```

```
txtstream.WriteLine("        display:inline-block;")
txtstream.WriteLine("        width: 100%;")
txtstream.WriteLine("   end;")
txtstream.WriteLine("   select")
txtstream.WriteLine("   begin")
txtstream.WriteLine("        COLOR: navy;")
txtstream.WriteLine("        FONT-FAMILY: font-family: Cambria, serif;")
txtstream.WriteLine("        FONT-SIZE: 10px;")
txtstream.WriteLine("        text-align: left;")
txtstream.WriteLine("        white-Space: nowrap;")
txtstream.WriteLine("        display:inline-block;")
txtstream.WriteLine("        width: 100%;")
txtstream.WriteLine("   end;")
txtstream.WriteLine("   input")
txtstream.WriteLine("   begin")
txtstream.WriteLine("        COLOR: navy;")
txtstream.WriteLine("        FONT-FAMILY: font-family: Cambria, serif;")
txtstream.WriteLine("        FONT-SIZE: 12px;")
txtstream.WriteLine("        text-align: left;")
txtstream.WriteLine("        display:table-cell;")
txtstream.WriteLine("        white-Space: nowrap;")
txtstream.WriteLine("   end;")
txtstream.WriteLine("   h1 begin")
txtstream.WriteLine("   color: antiquewhite;")
txtstream.WriteLine("   text-shadow: 1px 1px 1px black;")
txtstream.WriteLine("   padding: 3px;")
txtstream.WriteLine("   text-align: center;")
```

txtstream.WriteLine(" box-shadow: inset 2px 2px 5px rgba(0,0,0,0.5);, inset -2px -2px 5px rgba(255,255,255,0.5);;")

txtstream.WriteLine(" end;")

txtstream.WriteLine(" tr:nth-child(even);beginbackground-color:#f2f2f2;end;")

txtstream.WriteLine(" tr:nth-child(odd);beginbackground-color:#cccccc; color:#f2f2f2;end;")

txtstream.WriteLine(" </style>');

GHOST DECORATED

txtstream.WriteLine(" <style type='text/css'>');

txtstream.WriteLine(" th")

txtstream.WriteLine(" begin")

txtstream.WriteLine(" COLOR: black;")

txtstream.WriteLine(" BACKGROUND-COLOR: white;")

txtstream.WriteLine(" FONT-FAMILY:font-family: Cambria, serif;")

txtstream.WriteLine(" FONT-SIZE: 12px;")

txtstream.WriteLine(" text-align: left;")

txtstream.WriteLine(" white-Space: nowrap;")

txtstream.WriteLine(" end;")

txtstream.WriteLine(" td")

txtstream.WriteLine(" begin")

txtstream.WriteLine(" COLOR: black;")

txtstream.WriteLine(" BACKGROUND-COLOR: white;")

txtstream.WriteLine(" FONT-FAMILY: font-family: Cambria, serif;")

txtstream.WriteLine(" FONT-SIZE: 12px;")

txtstream.WriteLine(" text-align: left;")

txtstream.WriteLine(" white-Space: nowrap;")

```
txtstream.WriteLine("  end;")
txtstream.WriteLine("  div")
txtstream.WriteLine("  begin")
txtstream.WriteLine("    COLOR: black;")
txtstream.WriteLine("    BACKGROUND-COLOR: white;")
txtstream.WriteLine("    FONT-FAMILY: font-family: Cambria, serif;")
txtstream.WriteLine("    FONT-SIZE: 10px;")
txtstream.WriteLine("    text-align: left;")
txtstream.WriteLine("    white-Space: nowrap;")
txtstream.WriteLine("  end;")
txtstream.WriteLine("  span")
txtstream.WriteLine("  begin")
txtstream.WriteLine("    COLOR: black;")
txtstream.WriteLine("    BACKGROUND-COLOR: white;")
txtstream.WriteLine("    FONT-FAMILY: font-family: Cambria, serif;")
txtstream.WriteLine("    FONT-SIZE: 10px;")
txtstream.WriteLine("    text-align: left;")
txtstream.WriteLine("    white-Space: nowrap;")
txtstream.WriteLine("    display:inline-block;")
txtstream.WriteLine("    width: 100%;")
txtstream.WriteLine("  end;")
txtstream.WriteLine("  textarea")
txtstream.WriteLine("  begin")
txtstream.WriteLine("    COLOR: black;")
txtstream.WriteLine("    BACKGROUND-COLOR: white;")
txtstream.WriteLine("    FONT-FAMILY: font-family: Cambria, serif;")
txtstream.WriteLine("    FONT-SIZE: 10px;")
```

```
txtstream.WriteLine("        text-align: left;")
txtstream.WriteLine("        white-Space: nowrap;")
txtstream.WriteLine("        width: 100%;")
txtstream.WriteLine("    end;")
txtstream.WriteLine("    select")
txtstream.WriteLine("    begin")
txtstream.WriteLine("        COLOR: black;")
txtstream.WriteLine("        BACKGROUND-COLOR: white;")
txtstream.WriteLine("        FONT-FAMILY: font-family: Cambria, serif;")
txtstream.WriteLine("        FONT-SIZE: 10px;")
txtstream.WriteLine("        text-align: left;")
txtstream.WriteLine("        white-Space: nowrap;")
txtstream.WriteLine("        width: 100%;")
txtstream.WriteLine("    end;")
txtstream.WriteLine("    input")
txtstream.WriteLine("    begin")
txtstream.WriteLine("        COLOR: black;")
txtstream.WriteLine("        BACKGROUND-COLOR: white;")
txtstream.WriteLine("        FONT-FAMILY: font-family: Cambria, serif;")
txtstream.WriteLine("        FONT-SIZE: 12px;")
txtstream.WriteLine("        text-align: left;")
txtstream.WriteLine("        display:table-cell;")
txtstream.WriteLine("        white-Space: nowrap;")
txtstream.WriteLine("    end;")
txtstream.WriteLine("    h1 begin")
txtstream.WriteLine("    color: antiquewhite;")
txtstream.WriteLine("    text-shadow: 1px 1px 1px black;")
```

```
txtstream.WriteLine("    padding: 3px;")

txtstream.WriteLine("    text-align: center;")

txtstream.WriteLine("    box-shadow: inset 2px 2px 5px rgba(0,0,0,0.5);, inset -2px
-2px 5px rgba(255,255,255,0.5);;")

txtstream.WriteLine("    end;")

txtstream.WriteLine("    </style>');
```

3D


```
txtstream.WriteLine("    <style type='text/css'>');

txtstream.WriteLine("    body")

txtstream.WriteLine("    begin")

txtstream.WriteLine("        PADDING-RIGHT: 0px;")

txtstream.WriteLine("        PADDING-LEFT: 0px;")

txtstream.WriteLine("        PADDING-BOTTOM: 0px;")

txtstream.WriteLine("        MARGIN: 0px;")

txtstream.WriteLine("        COLOR: #333;")

txtstream.WriteLine("        PADDING-TOP: 0px;")

txtstream.WriteLine("        FONT-FAMILY: verdana, arial, helvetica, sans-serif;")

txtstream.WriteLine("    end;")

txtstream.WriteLine("    table")

txtstream.WriteLine("    begin")

txtstream.WriteLine("        BORDER-RIGHT: #999999 3px solid;")

txtstream.WriteLine("        PADDING-RIGHT: 6px;")

txtstream.WriteLine("        PADDING-LEFT: 6px;")

txtstream.WriteLine("        FONT-WEIGHT: Bold;")
```

txtstream.WriteLine("   FONT-SIZE: 14px;")

txtstream.WriteLine("   PADDING-BOTTOM: 6px;")

txtstream.WriteLine("   COLOR: Peru;")

txtstream.WriteLine("   LINE-HEIGHT: 14px;")

txtstream.WriteLine("   PADDING-TOP: 6px;")

txtstream.WriteLine("   BORDER-BOTTOM: #999 1px solid;")

txtstream.WriteLine("   BACKGROUND-COLOR: #eeeeee;")

txtstream.WriteLine("   FONT-FAMILY: verdana, arial, helvetica, sans-serif;")

txtstream.WriteLine("   FONT-SIZE: 12px;")

txtstream.WriteLine("   end;")

txtstream.WriteLine("   th")

txtstream.WriteLine("   begin")

txtstream.WriteLine("   BORDER-RIGHT: #999999 3px solid;")

txtstream.WriteLine("   PADDING-RIGHT: 6px;")

txtstream.WriteLine("   PADDING-LEFT: 6px;")

txtstream.WriteLine("   FONT-WEIGHT: Bold;")

txtstream.WriteLine("   FONT-SIZE: 14px;")

txtstream.WriteLine("   PADDING-BOTTOM: 6px;")

txtstream.WriteLine("   COLOR: darkred;")

txtstream.WriteLine("   LINE-HEIGHT: 14px;")

txtstream.WriteLine("   PADDING-TOP: 6px;")

txtstream.WriteLine("   BORDER-BOTTOM: #999 1px solid;")

txtstream.WriteLine("   BACKGROUND-COLOR: #eeeeee;")

txtstream.WriteLine("   FONT-FAMILY:font-family: Cambria, serif;")

txtstream.WriteLine("   FONT-SIZE: 12px;")

txtstream.WriteLine("   text-align: left;")

txtstream.WriteLine("   white-Space: nowrap;")

```
txtstream.WriteLine("   end;")

txtstream.WriteLine("   .th")

txtstream.WriteLine("   begin")

txtstream.WriteLine("      BORDER-RIGHT: #999999 2px solid;")

txtstream.WriteLine("      PADDING-RIGHT: 6px;")

txtstream.WriteLine("      PADDING-LEFT: 6px;")

txtstream.WriteLine("      FONT-WEIGHT: Bold;")

txtstream.WriteLine("      PADDING-BOTTOM: 6px;")

txtstream.WriteLine("      COLOR: black;")

txtstream.WriteLine("      PADDING-TOP: 6px;")

txtstream.WriteLine("      BORDER-BOTTOM: #999 2px solid;")

txtstream.WriteLine("      BACKGROUND-COLOR: #eeeeee;")

txtstream.WriteLine("      FONT-FAMILY: font-family: Cambria, serif;")

txtstream.WriteLine("      FONT-SIZE: 10px;")

txtstream.WriteLine("      text-align: right;")

txtstream.WriteLine("      white-Space: nowrap;")

txtstream.WriteLine("   end;")

txtstream.WriteLine("   td")

txtstream.WriteLine("   begin")

txtstream.WriteLine("      BORDER-RIGHT: #999999 3px solid;")

txtstream.WriteLine("      PADDING-RIGHT: 6px;")

txtstream.WriteLine("      PADDING-LEFT: 6px;")

txtstream.WriteLine("      FONT-WEIGHT: Normal;")

txtstream.WriteLine("      PADDING-BOTTOM: 6px;")

txtstream.WriteLine("      COLOR: navy;")

txtstream.WriteLine("      LINE-HEIGHT: 14px;")

txtstream.WriteLine("      PADDING-TOP: 6px;")
```

txtstream.WriteLine(" 　　　BORDER-BOTTOM: #999 1px solid;")

txtstream.WriteLine(" 　　　BACKGROUND-COLOR: #eeeeee;")

txtstream.WriteLine(" 　　　FONT-FAMILY: font-family: Cambria, serif;")

txtstream.WriteLine(" 　　　FONT-SIZE: 12px;")

txtstream.WriteLine(" 　　　text-align: left;")

txtstream.WriteLine(" 　　　white-Space: nowrap;")

txtstream.WriteLine(" 　end;")

txtstream.WriteLine(" 　div")

txtstream.WriteLine(" 　begin")

txtstream.WriteLine(" 　　　BORDER-RIGHT: #999999 3px solid;")

txtstream.WriteLine(" 　　　PADDING-RIGHT: 6px;")

txtstream.WriteLine(" 　　　PADDING-LEFT: 6px;")

txtstream.WriteLine(" 　　　FONT-WEIGHT: Normal;")

txtstream.WriteLine(" 　　　PADDING-BOTTOM: 6px;")

txtstream.WriteLine(" 　　　COLOR: white;")

txtstream.WriteLine(" 　　　PADDING-TOP: 6px;")

txtstream.WriteLine(" 　　　BORDER-BOTTOM: #999 1px solid;")

txtstream.WriteLine(" 　　　BACKGROUND-COLOR: navy;")

txtstream.WriteLine(" 　　　FONT-FAMILY: font-family: Cambria, serif;")

txtstream.WriteLine(" 　　　FONT-SIZE: 10px;")

txtstream.WriteLine(" 　　　text-align: left;")

txtstream.WriteLine(" 　　　white-Space: nowrap;")

txtstream.WriteLine(" 　end;")

txtstream.WriteLine(" 　span")

txtstream.WriteLine(" 　begin")

txtstream.WriteLine(" 　　　BORDER-RIGHT: #999999 3px solid;")

txtstream.WriteLine(" 　　　PADDING-RIGHT: 3px;")

```
txtstream.WriteLine("        PADDING-LEFT: 3px;")
txtstream.WriteLine("        FONT-WEIGHT: Normal;")
txtstream.WriteLine("        PADDING-BOTTOM: 3px;")
txtstream.WriteLine("        COLOR: white;")
txtstream.WriteLine("        PADDING-TOP: 3px;")
txtstream.WriteLine("        BORDER-BOTTOM: #999 1px solid;")
txtstream.WriteLine("        BACKGROUND-COLOR: navy;")
txtstream.WriteLine("        FONT-FAMILY: font-family: Cambria, serif;")
txtstream.WriteLine("        FONT-SIZE: 10px;")
txtstream.WriteLine("        text-align: left;")
txtstream.WriteLine("        white-Space: nowrap;")
txtstream.WriteLine("        display:inline-block;")
txtstream.WriteLine("        width: 100%;")
txtstream.WriteLine("    end;")
txtstream.WriteLine("    textarea")
txtstream.WriteLine("    begin")
txtstream.WriteLine("        BORDER-RIGHT: #999999 3px solid;")
txtstream.WriteLine("        PADDING-RIGHT: 3px;")
txtstream.WriteLine("        PADDING-LEFT: 3px;")
txtstream.WriteLine("        FONT-WEIGHT: Normal;")
txtstream.WriteLine("        PADDING-BOTTOM: 3px;")
txtstream.WriteLine("        COLOR: white;")
txtstream.WriteLine("        PADDING-TOP: 3px;")
txtstream.WriteLine("        BORDER-BOTTOM: #999 1px solid;")
txtstream.WriteLine("        BACKGROUND-COLOR: navy;")
txtstream.WriteLine("        FONT-FAMILY: font-family: Cambria, serif;")
txtstream.WriteLine("        FONT-SIZE: 10px;")
```

```
txtstream.WriteLine("      text-align: left;")
txtstream.WriteLine("      white-Space: nowrap;")
txtstream.WriteLine("      width: 100%;")
txtstream.WriteLine("   end;")
txtstream.WriteLine("   select")
txtstream.WriteLine("   begin")
txtstream.WriteLine("      BORDER-RIGHT: #999999 3px solid;")
txtstream.WriteLine("      PADDING-RIGHT: 6px;")
txtstream.WriteLine("      PADDING-LEFT: 6px;")
txtstream.WriteLine("      FONT-WEIGHT: Normal;")
txtstream.WriteLine("      PADDING-BOTTOM: 6px;")
txtstream.WriteLine("      COLOR: white;")
txtstream.WriteLine("      PADDING-TOP: 6px;")
txtstream.WriteLine("      BORDER-BOTTOM: #999 1px solid;")
txtstream.WriteLine("      BACKGROUND-COLOR: navy;")
txtstream.WriteLine("      FONT-FAMILY: font-family: Cambria, serif;")
txtstream.WriteLine("      FONT-SIZE: 10px;")
txtstream.WriteLine("      text-align: left;")
txtstream.WriteLine("      white-Space: nowrap;")
txtstream.WriteLine("      width: 100%;")
txtstream.WriteLine("   end;")
txtstream.WriteLine("   input")
txtstream.WriteLine("   begin")
txtstream.WriteLine("      BORDER-RIGHT: #999999 3px solid;")
txtstream.WriteLine("      PADDING-RIGHT: 3px;")
txtstream.WriteLine("      PADDING-LEFT: 3px;")
txtstream.WriteLine("      FONT-WEIGHT: Bold;")
```

```
txtstream.WriteLine("        PADDING-BOTTOM: 3px;")
txtstream.WriteLine("        COLOR: white;")
txtstream.WriteLine("        PADDING-TOP: 3px;")
txtstream.WriteLine("        BORDER-BOTTOM: #999 1px solid;")
txtstream.WriteLine("        BACKGROUND-COLOR: navy;")
txtstream.WriteLine("        FONT-FAMILY: font-family: Cambria, serif;")
txtstream.WriteLine("        FONT-SIZE: 12px;")
txtstream.WriteLine("        text-align: left;")
txtstream.WriteLine("        display:table-cell;")
txtstream.WriteLine("        white-Space: nowrap;")
txtstream.WriteLine("        width: 100%;")
txtstream.WriteLine("    end;")
txtstream.WriteLine("    h1 begin")
txtstream.WriteLine("    color: antiquewhite;")
txtstream.WriteLine("    text-shadow: 1px 1px 1px black;")
txtstream.WriteLine("    padding: 3px;")
txtstream.WriteLine("    text-align: center;")
txtstream.WriteLine("    box-shadow: inset 2px 2px 5px rgba(0,0,0,0.5);, inset -2px -2px 5px rgba(255,255,255,0.5);;")
txtstream.WriteLine("    end;")
txtstream.WriteLine("    </style>');
```

SHADOW BOX

```
txtstream.WriteLine("    <style type='text/css'>');
txtstream.WriteLine("   body")
txtstream.WriteLine("   begin")
```

txtstream.WriteLine("   PADDING-RIGHT: 0px;")

txtstream.WriteLine("   PADDING-LEFT: 0px;")

txtstream.WriteLine("   PADDING-BOTTOM: 0px;")

txtstream.WriteLine("   MARGIN: 0px;")

txtstream.WriteLine("   COLOR: #333;")

txtstream.WriteLine("   PADDING-TOP: 0px;")

txtstream.WriteLine("   FONT-FAMILY: verdana, arial, helvetica, sans-serif;")

txtstream.WriteLine("   end;")

txtstream.WriteLine("   table")

txtstream.WriteLine("   begin")

txtstream.WriteLine("   BORDER-RIGHT: #999999 1px solid;")

txtstream.WriteLine("   PADDING-RIGHT: 1px;")

txtstream.WriteLine("   PADDING-LEFT: 1px;")

txtstream.WriteLine("   PADDING-BOTTOM: 1px;")

txtstream.WriteLine("   LINE-HEIGHT: 8px;")

txtstream.WriteLine("   PADDING-TOP: 1px;")

txtstream.WriteLine("   BORDER-BOTTOM: #999 1px solid;")

txtstream.WriteLine("   BACKGROUND-COLOR: #eeeeee;")

txtstream.WriteLine("   filter:progid:DXImageTransform.Microsoft.Shadow(color='silver', Direction=135, Strength=16")

txtstream.WriteLine("   end;")

txtstream.WriteLine("   th")

txtstream.WriteLine("   begin")

txtstream.WriteLine("   BORDER-RIGHT: #999999 3px solid;")

txtstream.WriteLine("   PADDING-RIGHT: 6px;")

txtstream.WriteLine("   PADDING-LEFT: 6px;")

txtstream.WriteLine("   FONT-WEIGHT: Bold;")

```
txtstream.WriteLine("        FONT-SIZE: 14px;")

txtstream.WriteLine("        PADDING-BOTTOM: 6px;")

txtstream.WriteLine("        COLOR: darkred;")

txtstream.WriteLine("        LINE-HEIGHT: 14px;")

txtstream.WriteLine("        PADDING-TOP: 6px;")

txtstream.WriteLine("        BORDER-BOTTOM: #999 1px solid;")

txtstream.WriteLine("        BACKGROUND-COLOR: #eeeeee;")

txtstream.WriteLine("        FONT-FAMILY: font-family: Cambria, serif;")

txtstream.WriteLine("        FONT-SIZE: 12px;")

txtstream.WriteLine("        text-align: left;")

txtstream.WriteLine("        white-Space: nowrap;")

txtstream.WriteLine("    end;")

txtstream.WriteLine("  .th")

txtstream.WriteLine("  begin")

txtstream.WriteLine("        BORDER-RIGHT: #999999 2px solid;")

txtstream.WriteLine("        PADDING-RIGHT: 6px;")

txtstream.WriteLine("        PADDING-LEFT: 6px;")

txtstream.WriteLine("        FONT-WEIGHT: Bold;")

txtstream.WriteLine("        PADDING-BOTTOM: 6px;")

txtstream.WriteLine("        COLOR: black;")

txtstream.WriteLine("        PADDING-TOP: 6px;")

txtstream.WriteLine("        BORDER-BOTTOM: #999 2px solid;")

txtstream.WriteLine("        BACKGROUND-COLOR: #eeeeee;")

txtstream.WriteLine("        FONT-FAMILY: font-family: Cambria, serif;")

txtstream.WriteLine("        FONT-SIZE: 10px;")

txtstream.WriteLine("        text-align: right;")

txtstream.WriteLine("        white-Space: nowrap;")
```

txtstream.WriteLine("   end;")

txtstream.WriteLine(" td")

txtstream.WriteLine(" begin")

txtstream.WriteLine("   BORDER-RIGHT: #999999 3px solid;")

txtstream.WriteLine("   PADDING-RIGHT: 6px;")

txtstream.WriteLine("   PADDING-LEFT: 6px;")

txtstream.WriteLine("   FONT-WEIGHT: Normal;")

txtstream.WriteLine("   PADDING-BOTTOM: 6px;")

txtstream.WriteLine("   COLOR: navy;")

txtstream.WriteLine("   LINE-HEIGHT: 14px;")

txtstream.WriteLine("   PADDING-TOP: 6px;")

txtstream.WriteLine("   BORDER-BOTTOM: #999 1px solid;")

txtstream.WriteLine("   BACKGROUND-COLOR: #eeeeee;")

txtstream.WriteLine("   FONT-FAMILY: font-family: Cambria, serif;")

txtstream.WriteLine("   FONT-SIZE: 12px;")

txtstream.WriteLine("   text-align: left;")

txtstream.WriteLine("   white-Space: nowrap;")

txtstream.WriteLine("   end;")

txtstream.WriteLine(" div")

txtstream.WriteLine(" begin")

txtstream.WriteLine("   BORDER-RIGHT: #999999 3px solid;")

txtstream.WriteLine("   PADDING-RIGHT: 6px;")

txtstream.WriteLine("   PADDING-LEFT: 6px;")

txtstream.WriteLine("   FONT-WEIGHT: Normal;")

txtstream.WriteLine("   PADDING-BOTTOM: 6px;")

txtstream.WriteLine("   COLOR: white;")

txtstream.WriteLine("   PADDING-TOP: 6px;")

```
txtstream.WriteLine("            BORDER-BOTTOM: #999 1px solid;")
txtstream.WriteLine("            BACKGROUND-COLOR: navy;")
txtstream.WriteLine("            FONT-FAMILY: font-family: Cambria, serif;")
txtstream.WriteLine("            FONT-SIZE: 10px;")
txtstream.WriteLine("            text-align: left;")
txtstream.WriteLine("            white-Space: nowrap;")
txtstream.WriteLine("        end;")
txtstream.WriteLine("        span")
txtstream.WriteLine("        begin")
txtstream.WriteLine("            BORDER-RIGHT: #999999 3px solid;")
txtstream.WriteLine("            PADDING-RIGHT: 3px;")
txtstream.WriteLine("            PADDING-LEFT: 3px;")
txtstream.WriteLine("            FONT-WEIGHT: Normal;")
txtstream.WriteLine("            PADDING-BOTTOM: 3px;")
txtstream.WriteLine("            COLOR: white;")
txtstream.WriteLine("            PADDING-TOP: 3px;")
txtstream.WriteLine("            BORDER-BOTTOM: #999 1px solid;")
txtstream.WriteLine("            BACKGROUND-COLOR: navy;")
txtstream.WriteLine("            FONT-FAMILY: font-family: Cambria, serif;")
txtstream.WriteLine("            FONT-SIZE: 10px;")
txtstream.WriteLine("            text-align: left;")
txtstream.WriteLine("            white-Space: nowrap;")
txtstream.WriteLine("            display: inline-block;")
txtstream.WriteLine("            width: 100%;")
txtstream.WriteLine("        end;")
txtstream.WriteLine("        textarea")
txtstream.WriteLine("        begin")
```

```
txtstream.WriteLine("        BORDER-RIGHT: #999999 3px solid;")
txtstream.WriteLine("        PADDING-RIGHT: 3px;")
txtstream.WriteLine("        PADDING-LEFT: 3px;")
txtstream.WriteLine("        FONT-WEIGHT: Normal;")
txtstream.WriteLine("        PADDING-BOTTOM: 3px;")
txtstream.WriteLine("        COLOR: white;")
txtstream.WriteLine("        PADDING-TOP: 3px;")
txtstream.WriteLine("        BORDER-BOTTOM: #999 1px solid;")
txtstream.WriteLine("        BACKGROUND-COLOR: navy;")
txtstream.WriteLine("        FONT-FAMILY: font-family: Cambria, serif;")
txtstream.WriteLine("        FONT-SIZE: 10px;")
txtstream.WriteLine("        text-align: left;")
txtstream.WriteLine("        white-Space: nowrap;")
txtstream.WriteLine("        width: 100%;")
txtstream.WriteLine("    end;")
txtstream.WriteLine("    select")
txtstream.WriteLine("    begin")
txtstream.WriteLine("        BORDER-RIGHT: #999999 3px solid;")
txtstream.WriteLine("        PADDING-RIGHT: 6px;")
txtstream.WriteLine("        PADDING-LEFT: 6px;")
txtstream.WriteLine("        FONT-WEIGHT: Normal;")
txtstream.WriteLine("        PADDING-BOTTOM: 6px;")
txtstream.WriteLine("        COLOR: white;")
txtstream.WriteLine("        PADDING-TOP: 6px;")
txtstream.WriteLine("        BORDER-BOTTOM: #999 1px solid;")
txtstream.WriteLine("        BACKGROUND-COLOR: navy;")
txtstream.WriteLine("        FONT-FAMILY: font-family: Cambria, serif;")
```

```
txtstream.WriteLine("        FONT-SIZE: 10px;")

txtstream.WriteLine("        text-align: left;")

txtstream.WriteLine("        white-Space: nowrap;")

txtstream.WriteLine("        width: 100%;")

txtstream.WriteLine("    end;")

txtstream.WriteLine("    input")

txtstream.WriteLine("    begin")

txtstream.WriteLine("        BORDER-RIGHT: #999999 3px solid;")

txtstream.WriteLine("        PADDING-RIGHT: 3px;")

txtstream.WriteLine("        PADDING-LEFT: 3px;")

txtstream.WriteLine("        FONT-WEIGHT: Bold;")

txtstream.WriteLine("        PADDING-BOTTOM: 3px;")

txtstream.WriteLine("        COLOR: white;")

txtstream.WriteLine("        PADDING-TOP: 3px;")

txtstream.WriteLine("        BORDER-BOTTOM: #999 1px solid;")

txtstream.WriteLine("        BACKGROUND-COLOR: navy;")

txtstream.WriteLine("        FONT-FAMILY: font-family: Cambria, serif;")

txtstream.WriteLine("        FONT-SIZE: 12px;")

txtstream.WriteLine("        text-align: left;")

txtstream.WriteLine("        display: table-cell;")

txtstream.WriteLine("        white-Space: nowrap;")

txtstream.WriteLine("        width: 100%;")

txtstream.WriteLine("    end;")

txtstream.WriteLine("    h1 begin")

txtstream.WriteLine("    color: antiquewhite;")

txtstream.WriteLine("    text-shadow: 1px 1px 1px black;")

txtstream.WriteLine("    padding: 3px;")
```

```
txtstream.WriteLine("   text-align: center;")

txtstream.WriteLine("   box-shadow: inset 2px 2px 5px rgba(0,0,0,0.5);, inset -2px
-2px 5px rgba(255,255,255,0.5);;")

txtstream.WriteLine("   end;")

txtstream.WriteLine("   </style>');
```

www.ingramcontent.com/pod-product-compliance
Lightning Source LLC
Chambersburg PA
CBHW070843070326
40690CB00009B/1667